DREAM and CULTURE

DREAM and CULTURE

An Anthropological Study
of the Western Intellectual Tradition

SUSAN PARMAN

New York
Westport, Connecticut
London

Library of Congress Cataloging-in-Publication Data

Parman, Susan.
    Dream and culture : an anthropological study of the western
intellectual tradition / Susan Parman.
        p.   cm.
    Includes bibliographical references (p.   ) and index.
    ISBN 0-275-93230-3 (alk. paper)
    1. Dreams—History. 2. Civilization, Occidental—Psychological
aspects. 3. Europe—Intellectual life.   I. Title.
    BF1078.P32   1991
    306.4—dc20   90-7459

British Library Cataloguing in Publication Data is available.

Library of Congress Catalog Card Number: 90-7459
ISBN: 0-275-93230-3

First published in 1991

Praeger Publishers, One Madison Avenue, New York, NY 10010
An imprint of Greenwood Publishing Group, Inc.

Printed in the United States of America

The paper used in this book complies with the
Permanent Paper Standard issued by the National
Information Standards Organization (Z39.48-1984).

10 9 8 7 6 5 4 3 2 1

I dedicate this book to my husband, Jacob Pandian, without whose corporeal, spiritual, and intellectual support this book would not exist. He remained calm while I laughed maniacally over *The Romance of the Mushroom* and *Almond*, nurtured the household when I forgot that humans have bodies as well as souls, played Virgil to my Dante and St. Augustine to my Petrarch, and above all provided the philosopher's stone to my transmutation of the brain-based dream into a cultural system. His is truly a voice of transcendent realism.

Oneiros (Greek), divinatory dream-figure sent by the gods to deliver a message.

Dream (English), from Old Saxon *drom*, mirth, minstrelsy. According to Skeat (1961), the sense of "vision" is not found in the earliest English. He suggests comparison with German *trug-bild*, a phantom, and German *trugen*, to deceive. Dream as a verb appears in the thirteenth century, with dream as subject; the verb derived from the noun, as in German *traumen*, to dream, from *traum*.

-eni- (Kalapalo Indians of central Brazil), to dream, one of several intransitive verb forms describing a process rather than a discrete event (Basso 1987).

Contents

Preface

The dream is the ultimate cultural Rorschach. Universal in occurrence among humans and other mammals, it stems from a nonsymbolic surge of arousal from the brainstem that splays the cerebrum with fireworks. In humans these random fireworks are interpreted by the neocortex and given symbolic shape, in both idiosyncratic and culturally shared patterns. The dream is like an onion, constantly being peeled, but with endless layers. This book is about the epistemological layers of the dream in Western culture.

As used in this book, "Western culture" refers to epistemological structures of thought and meaning that are identified today as central to and distinctive of what is variously identified as "Western civilization," "the West," "the Western tradition."

I am using the term "culture" not in the sense of an ethnographic description of the holistic, integrated way of life of a particular ethnic, regional, or national population (as is usually described in ethnographies), but in a way that is more closely linked to the tradition of A. L. Kroeber (1944), Eric Wolf (1982), Michel Foucault (1972), and others, as dominant patterns of knowledge, configurations, world views, central themes, paradigms, and epistemes.

The patterns of "Western culture" were created in the philosophical writings of the Greeks and Romans; the writings of the Christian Church fathers; the literary, scientific, and artistic discourse that has developed, especially after the introduction of the printing press, from the Renaissance to the present day. These patterns serve as paradigms or vehicles to explain what it means to be human and to interpret the place of humankind in the universe. Despite local variations in customs, class, language, economics, and politics, it is possible to demarcate commonly used patterns of understanding, or systems of symbols, by which participants in "Western culture" or the "Western intellectual tradition" made sense of their world.   This book explores the uses of the dream in these systems of symbols, as epistemological configurations that changed over time.

The theoretical framework of culture used in this book derives from the contributions of many scholars and many related disciplines concerned with the study of knowledge and meaning systems.   Symbolic anthropology (especially the writings of Clifford Geertz, Victor Turner, E. E. Evans-Pritchard, and Mary Douglas), semiotics, cultural poetics, cultural criticism, historical ethnography, and literary theory (see Eagleton 1983; Clifford and Marcus 1986) have, in recent times, made significant advances in our understanding of culture. Using these disciplines as a point of reference, culture may be defined as a system of communication that may be analyzed as an ongoing dialogue whose purpose is to create and maintain meaning. The interpretation of culture as a system of communication does not contradict the anthropological models of culture as "superorganic" units or entities composed of established, well-bounded, stable rules that guide behavior, but focuses on understanding the processes involved in the creation and maintenance of culture. As Mary Douglas and Aaron Wildavsky suggest,

> Instead of the old recurrent imagery of knowledge as a solid thing, bounded or mapped out, we prefer the idea of knowledge as the changing product of social activity. . . . It has been compared to an open-ended communal enterprise, to a ship voyaging to an unknown destination but never arriving and never dropping anchor. It is like a many-sided conversation in which being ultimately right or wrong is not at issue.   What matters is that the conversation continue with new definitions and solutions and terms made deep enough to hold the meanings being tried (1982:192-3).

Culture is a changing cluster of symbols, a set of understandings that constantly changes its references as it adapts to new conditions; it is a historical orchestra. And in the effort to "hold the meanings being tried," the players in the orchestra strive to strike memorable keys, to create significant symbols, metaphors, and myths to integrate past, present, and future in an integrated whole. This whole constitutes a system of meaning, or repertoire of symbols developed through interaction with the environment, which may be called culture.

Culture is based on the human capacity to symbolize. All symbols are entities that stand for something else, but some symbols are heavier, more resonant, and more significant than others. Because of their multiple referents and complex associations, these symbols signify more to the users. Variously labeled "significant symbols," "core symbols," "sacred symbols," "master symbols," "dominant symbols," and "key symbols," they provide conceptual and motivational models for human thought and action. They constitute cultural systems which integrate a diversity of symbols and enable people to make sense of their world and to motivate and direct their behavior (see Parman 1990).

An analogy may be made with a keyboard on a piano. The keys are symbols; the melodies, harmonic progressions, *etudes* and *opi* (simple and complex) are culture created, culture-in-action. People are constantly playing melodies; humans are constantly creating connections between symbols, patterns of symbolic progression, and symphonies of meaning. The dream is one key. Sometimes that key is played, drawn into a line of melody, or connected to other keys; sometimes it is not played at all.

How is the dream played in Western culture? What meanings do we make of it? What connections do we create with other symbol keys? The dream key has been played over and over again in Western culture; it is a richly evocative, resonant symbol. This book is about the playing of the dream key in Western culture, or, in the language of semiotic anthropology, about its semantics, syntactics, and pragmatics (its meanings, linkages, and uses).

Throughout Western cultural history, the dream has posed a challenge to whatever epistemological fashion is in vogue. The dream has been a sleep-time visitor, an allegorical translation of the unknowable divinity, an illusion distracting us from the exercise of pure Reason, or a source of poetic inspiration. In psychoanalysis the dream became a "royal road to the unconscious," revealing unresolved individual and cultural contradictions. My concern in this book is to investigate and interpret the diverse epistemological fashions that have been used in the representations of the dream in Western culture.

My interest in dreams began when I was an undergraduate at Antioch College. As part of the college work-study program, I became a "normal volunteer" at the National Institutes of Health in Bethesda, Maryland. I was recruited first as a subject and then as a volunteer researcher in physiological dream experiments being conducted by Fred Snyder and J. Allan Hobson of NIH. The dream studies done by E. Aserinsky and N. Kleitman at the University of Chicago during the 1950s, which measured the electroencephalographic output of the brain during sleep (EEG), had stimulated an array of scientific research that, instead of being concerned with the complex symbolism of dreams in a psychoanalytic framework, examined the dream as a cyclical biological process. The questions asked included: What happened to respiration and heart rate during the stages of sleep? What were dream reports like when you woke someone up at different times of the night? Fred Snyder, the head of the dream laboratory at NIH, was a quiet man who was endlessly tinkering with methods of measuring various physiological dimensions. Allan Hobson was restless, thoughtful, and intensely curious about the meaning of the squiggles that filled the mountains of EEG paper that accumulated during the course of the experiments. He was a natural teacher in both the science of dreams and general biology. I returned to Antioch College and, with a strong background in the humanities, majored in psychology with an interest and some training in neurophysiology. Although I went on to graduate school in anthropology (a nice compromise for someone with strong interests in both the sciences and humanities), over the years I developed an evolutionary theory of dreaming (see Parman 1979) that, in its nonsymbolic, non-human-centered focus on cycles of arousal, resembles the theory developed by Hobson and Robert McCarley at Harvard during the past few years (see Hobson and McCarley 1977), except that it links dreaming with information theory and epilepsy. I would like nothing better than to spend the next five years studying the phylogeny of epilepsy and its relationship to dreaming sleep.

Thus, my primary interest in dreaming is evolutionary, scientific, and nonsymbolic. I say this to make clear a fundamental premise of this book: I am committed to empirical reality, both philosophically and practically. My interest in symbols and the interpretation of symbols is to understand them in their historical, contextual setting. The symbolic creations of human beings are endlessly fascinating; but, like dreams, they often lend themselves to interpretations that tell more about the interpretive orientation of the interpreter than about the phenomenon itself. One can focus scientifically on interpretation (that is, try to put it in context as it is rather than how you want it to be) at the same time that you realize that the equipment with which you are observing and thinking is part of the phenomenon. But the framework of science, with its assumptions of testability and commitment to phenomenon as object rather than subject is, as science should be, useful, practical and down-to-earth. It helps us learn more about the world; it is the best thing we have for telling us what is, rather than what we would like to exist. Like Sigismund of Life's a Dream, I sometimes find it difficult to tell whether my theories are "dream or reality," illusory or of-the-world; but I know they are different from the allegorical dream visions of the Middle Ages, and I hope that they will enable us to put the dream (that in California, in particular, is often put to bizarre interpretive uses) in cultural perspective.

1

The Cultural Uses
of Dreams

THE DREAM AS A CULTURAL SYSTEM

This book is an anthropological and historical investigation of the conceptions of the dream (its meanings, connections with other ideas, and uses) in Western culture from Greco-Roman times to the present. I offer an analysis of how dream experiences were formulated in a culturally meaningful manner and how these formulations were linked with other aspects of culture at different periods in the Western tradition.

Dreaming is a universal biopsychological process that has been studied from multiple points of view. Biologists examine its evolutionary significance, the correlation of physiological changes such as heart rate and respiration with stages of sleep, the investigation of structures in the brainstem which are activated during Stage I rapid-eye-movement (REM) dreaming sleep, the adaptive significance of REM, periodic arousal, and intense cortical activity during sleep, and so on. Psychologists analyze the cognitive and emotional significance of dream symbolism for the individual dreamer, and the contribution of the dream to understanding sensory, associative, emotive, or arousal models of the mind. Parapsychologists investigate its potential as an extrasensory mode of communication, artists its creative possibilities, and anthropologists the cross-cultural configurations of meaning in which it has been cast. Cultural interpretations of dreams include the view of dreams as "intentional messages, i.e. culturally defined means of communication" (Fabian 1966:560), as text (Ricoeur 1970), or as cultural systems composed of interconnected symbols (Parman 1983, Mannheim 1987). Cultures everywhere have words to describe it. Variously classified as divinatory, deceitful, experiential, deriving from sensory experience, otherworldly, preposterous, mad, or mirthful, dreaming is a distinctive experience.

"But what does it *mean*?" I was asked when I once proposed teaching a multidisciplinary course on dreams. "What is the truth about dreams?" The position taken in this book is anthropological: truth is contextual, depending on the uses to which the dream is put in a society. The dream is culturally embedded, part of a system of symbols. It may, biologically, be linked with cycles of arousal that are part of a mammalian pattern that precede the development of a cerebral cortex sufficiently complex to make culture possible; but the meaning attributed to it by a culture may ignore arousal and emphasize external messages from the gods. In this book, the question "What does a dream mean" gets a hermeneutic answer: it means what it means.

One person examining my course proposal was disturbed by the number of approaches I was using. A traditional Freudian, he had read an anthropological treatise that seemed to support his assumption that "the truth" about dreams was that the dream constituted the "royal road" to the unconscious mind. I replied that the anthropologist, A. F. C. Wallace (1969), had described the dream symbology of the Iroquois of the seventeenth and eighteenth centuries that was remarkably similar to the dream symbology of middle-class Westerners of the late-nineteenth and early twentieth centuries, but that did not "prove" the universal validity of Freudian theory.

The Iroquois of the seventeenth and eighteenth centuries saw the dream experience as central to their understanding of human nature and divinity and as a source of guidance "in all the important affairs of life" (Wallace 1969:59). They believed that:

> our souls have . . . desires, which are, as it were, inborn and con-
> cealed . . . when these desires are accomplished, it is satisfied; but
> on the contrary, if it [the soul] be not granted what it desires, it be-
> comes angry, and . . . often it also revolts against the body, causing
> various diseases, and even death. (Father Ragueneau, 1649, quoted
> by Wallace 1969: 59)

Despite the intriguing similarities between the Iroquois and Freudian interpretation of dreams, there are important differences that are explainable not by researching whether the Iroquois or Freud had the "more correct" model of the unconscious but by looking at the two cultures in which the dream is used. Iroquois dream theory combined what Freudians call wish-fulfillment and what the Greeks described as *oneirocritica* (the dream as a divine visitor). The Iroquois took their dreams very seriously, and interpreted them as the wishes of supernatural beings, or as enactments of personal fate that they were destined to fulfill, whether the dream involved bathing in the middle of the night, engaging in sexual intercourse, murdering a Frenchman, traveling long distances to buy a dog, or being burned and tortured. Dreams became an avenue of dealing with social and cultural change, a vehicle by which a reorganized response to stress could be effectively mobilized. The dreamer became transformed into a prophet or messiah whose suggestions for change could be accepted. In this manner, a drunken Iroquois named Handsome Lake founded a revitalization movement, the "Old Way of Handsome Lake," that enabled the Iroquois to stop drinking, have men work in the fields instead of hunting and raiding, and be more receptive to Christianity. In Western culture, in contrast, Freudian psychoanalysis has been used to enable individuals to discover the creative fountainhead of their egotistical selves--to become daimonic shamans (see chapter 7).

THE DREAM IN WESTERN CULTURE

This book explores the cultural contexts in which dreams acquired relevance in the West as significant representations or symbols that were linked with symbols of divinity, health, knowledge, power, and so on. In other words, at different periods in Western history, the dream became linked with a diversity of religious, political, and ethnic symbols and functioned as a system of knowledge that validated or legitimized the social order. This book investigates how the phenomenon of dreaming has, at different periods in the history of Western culture, acquired relevance as a significant system of symbols and how it has been linked with other significant symbols in the Western tradition.

For convenience, I delineate periods within the history of the Western tradition with reference to the dominant intellectual currents of Europe and the European settlements outside of Europe (see "Historical Periods").

BIOPSYCHOLOGICAL VERSUS CULTURAL
FORMULATIONS: ANOTHER EXAMPLE

You will never find the city of your dreams until you starve.
Hesiod quoted by Patience Gray,
Honey from a Weed

All humans are required, biologically, to eat; but "food" is a cultural construct as well as a biological necessity. What meanings, connections, and practice do humans create through the social construction of the biological ingestion of food? In the film *Babette's Feast* (1989), the general who realized that "all things are possible" because he was served the best meal he had ever eaten in an obscure village in the Danish wilds would not recognize a biological description of the process of digestion as an adequate description of the meal he had eaten. He was not eating proteins and carbohydrates but symbols of *communitas*, hope, and redemption.

As Peggy Sanday argues in *Divine Hunter: Cannibalism as a Cultural System* (1986), cannibalism is not about the biology of hunger but the symbolism of being. "The somatically based ritual symbols of cannibalism stamp the psyche and the social order in ritual acts that transform inchoate psychic energy, formulate self- and social-consciousness, and in some cases, transmit vital essence into social categories" (xii). Just as the general ate himself into a state of meaningful existence in *Babette's Feast*, Western culture has, for the past two thousand years, been dreaming itself into various states of existence.

If we based our decisions of what and how much to eat solely on the basis of calories and the calculus of biochemical needs, we would as easily consume camels, hares and rock badgers as we do cattle; but, as Mary Douglas has argued in her book *Purity and Danger* (1966), the "abominations of Leviticus" are not bundles of botulism but entities that either confuse or fall outside cultural categories. In the Judeo-Christian biblical scheme of the world, creatures are assigned either to earth, water, or air, and each has its appropriate features and form of locomotion. Any violation of expected features or habitation, for instance, four-footed creatures flying; two-handed creatures like the mole who are perversely quadrupedal instead of bipedal; eels and worms that swim in the sea but have no fins or scales; and so on, renders a creature ritually unclean.

In the same way, the definition of a dream as a random splay of excitation in cortical neurons arising from the reticular formation would strike most members of a Western audience as being relatively uninteresting or outside of the normal significance attributed to dreaming. Dreams signify; they connote rich, dense bouquets of meaning. The significations of dreams are cultural, and the study of such significations can serve as a kind of cultural key to help us understand Western cultural assumptions about humankind, social order, and so on.

SOME EXAMPLES OF THE USES OF DREAMS
IN WESTERN CULTURE

A random perusal of books and articles that use "dreams" to convey a message opens a door to Western culture. *Dream Maker: The Rise and Fall of John Z. DeLorean* by Ivan Fallon and James Srodes (1983) is not only about the "dream car" (as the DMC-12 was called), but about the "American dream" of excessive riches and fame and the dangers of success. "The Dream Takes a Dark Shape," begins the first chapter of their book, and the authors suggest that they will reveal "how far we are willing to go to have our dreams fulfilled" as well as "the limitations of the institutions that we have established to protect our dreams" (Fallon and Srodes 1983:1).

The Pursuit of a Dream by Janet Sharp Hermann (1981), echoing the 20th-century "I have a dream" speech of Martin Luther King (1963), is about the collaboration of Confederate president Jefferson Davis's brother with a former slave to build an all-black utopian community in post-Civil War Mississippi.

"How the Wise Men Brought Malaria to Africa: And Other Cautionary Tales of Human Dreams and Opportunistic Mosquitoes" (Desowitz 1976) uses "dream" to symbolize humans setting themselves apart from nature.

Walker Chapman's book *The Golden Dream* (1967) begins, "The quest for El Dorado was an enterprise of fantasy that obsessed the adventurers of Europe for more than a century . . . their deeds constitute a monument to futility as well as an epic of high adventure." The use of the symbol "dream" enables the author to connote fantasy, utopia, and danger, with a hint of madness and death.

The Language of the Night: Essays on Fantasy and Science Fiction is a collection of writings by Ursula K. Le Guin (1979). In one essay, "Dreams Must Explain Themselves," she describes the creative process. She says that imagination is like a kingdom she "discovers" without conscious planning. "I am not an engineer, but an explorer. I discovered Earthsea." She ends the article with the statement, "It is the end of the trilogy, but it is the dream I have not stopped dreaming," the only explicit reference to "dream" in the entire chapter. Here "dream" is associated with the spatial dimensions of the imagination, with the subconscious or unconscious, with powerful forces that move independent of conscious volition or control.

The dream is used frequently by science fiction writers, and reflects the twentieth-century Freudian synthesis of scientific and romantic conceptions of the mind described in this book. In "Wings Out of Shadow" (Saberhagen 1983), humans fight the alien machines called "berserkers" which, like Hal the computer-gone-bad of *2001: A Space Odyssey* (1968), are the Rationalists's worst nightmare of scientific achievement. Saberhagen's human heroes, like the Romantics, fight the "berserkers" while they are in a dream state:

> No man could direct a ship or a weapon with anything like the competence of a good machine. The creeping slowness of human nerve impulses and of conscious thought disqualified humans from maintaining direct control of their ships in any space flight against berserkers. But the human subconscious was not so limited.

> Certain of its processes could not be correlated with any specific synaptic activity within the brain, and some theorists held that these processes took place outside of time. (Saberhagen 1983: 179)

The ability of the dreamer to transcend time and space, the limits of the body and rational logic, is an attribute of the daimonic shaman that emerged in the context of Western culture. In Western psychoanalysis, the dreamer learns, with his shamanic helper, the psychiatrist, to walk the dark side of his mind; and fiction, in particular science fiction, gives visual form to this world. In the film *Dreamscape* (1984), science in the form of a sleep laboratory opens the door to this magical other world, enabling dreamers to enter each other's dreams and, like gods, to either save or to destroy.

The dream as a bridge over which adventurous travelers can pass is quite different from the dream as an allegory of culture. For example, I would consider *Indiana Jones and the Last Crusade* (1989) to be the equivalent of Dante's *Divine Comedy* as an allegorical dream vision. In his quest for the Holy Grail, the hero, appropriately an archaeologist, is excavating the encyclopaedic icons of the Western tradition. He is not pursuing his own quest but, like Dante, traversing the landscape of Western culture and thereby serving an important didactic function.

THE INTEGRATION OF THE OTHER IN THE WESTERN TRADITION THROUGH DREAM SYMBOLOGY

> *the tendency of dreams to reveal the opposite or other-self of the person in waking life.*
>
> R. L. Megroz, *The Dream World*

In Western culture today, an important function of the dream is to integrate symbols of otherness. It connotes an underworld of the abnormal, immoral, aboriginal, nontemporal--a bridge to spirituality as conceived in various forms, conceptions of human potential, apocalyptic visions and utopia, and numerous other associations. Elements of this *episteme*, or systematic mode of knowing, may be traced to Greek times (see Dodds 1951), but it became a vital part of religious conceptions with the establishment of the Judeo-Christian tradition. Jacob Pandian (1985) argues that the Judeo-Christian orientation in the West established a mythological charter for bifurcating the self into two parts, the true and the untrue self.

All religious orientations provide symbolic vehicles for conceptualizing the self by representing human potential or possibilities of being; but while some represent and legitimize the diverse, contradictory aspects of human existence, others present a restricted, absolutist conception of human possibility.

Like the dramatic personae of a play of life, the mythological figures of a religious system may resolve the paradoxes of existence by combining in their representations the contradictory extremes of human possibility: They may be, at the same time, "good and evil, sexual and puritanical, wild and gentle, life-giving and death-giving" (Pandian 1985:49). For example, among the Greeks, divine beings:

> explored the nature of good and evil, virtue and debasement, maleness and femaleness, often depicting the coexistence of opposites in the same divine figure. . . . Gorgons, one-eyed witches, giants, heroes who were sometimes cowardly, bad kings who were also good, false wives who were sometimes true--the strange, the abnormal, the bad as well as the good, were all incorporated in a representation of the self. (Pandian 1985:9)

In Hinduism the god Siva, characterized by Wendy O'Flaherty (1973) as an "erotic ascetic," is a symbol both of "excessive sexuality and repressed sexuality, self-abandonment and total self-denial" (Pandian 1985:49).

In other societies, mythological figures may represent for their audience a narrower, more restricted conception of the self, for example, as only good, strong, pure, righteous, truthful, orderly, and perfect. Such a figure is the Christian god:

> The god of Christians is a representation of maleness, perfection, omnipotence, etc. Man is symbolized as created in the image of god. The discrepancy between the perfect god and his imperfect creation is explain in various myths that narrate the fall of man, original sin, salvation, grace, etc. The human experiences and characteristics that cannot be conceptualized with reference to god are identified as evil or abnormal and rejected as aspects of the self not connected with god. Thus a contrast between the true self and the untrue self is made, a contrast which is homologous to the contrast between grace and sin, orthodoxy and heresy, normal and abnormal, goodness and evil, holy and unholy, true knowledge and blasphemy, and so on. . . . (Pandian 1985:42)

Jung commented in his autobiography that he was amazed to find that Chinese and Hindus "are able to integrate so-called evil without losing face. In the West we cannot do this. . . . To the Oriental, good and evil are meaningfully contained in nature, and are merely varying degrees of the same thing" (1963:276).

The Judeo-Christian symbol of divinity, as a mythological charter or symbolic vehicle for Western man to conceptualize the self, establishes a dichotomy between those aspects of human behavior and existence which correspond to the mythological representation, and those which do not. In other words, human life as we know it (full of suffering and thoughtless deeds, forgetfulness and active connivance as well as altruism and friendship, good intentions and wise actions) may be divided into categories: those behaviors which represent the "true self," and those behaviors which represent the "untrue self." The establishment of such an absolutist contrast in the conception of the self requires mediating processes which can integrate excluded aspects into a comprehensive understanding of the whole of human existence. Once this dichotomy and a system of conceptual resolution are established, this way of thinking or knowing (this episteme or cultural system) can be used to interpret other phenomena, including the dream. If God is good, we require a repository of evil, the excluded aspects of the self. If man is defined as rational, how does he explain the irrational aspects of existence? Perhaps he invents irrational, primitive, childlike, "dreaming" people (the primitive) or an evolutionary, layer-cake model of the psyche.

Pandian uses this thesis to define the significance of anthropology in the Western tradition. He argues that as scholarship was secularized during the Renaissance with the humanistic revival of learning and as new lands were colonized, anthropology emerged as a vehicle for epistemic mediation. On the one hand anthropology created the non-Western other onto which aspects of the untrue self were projected (for example, as savage, ahistorical, cannibalistic); on the other hand it achieved a unified vision of humanity. Anthropology's role is to go to the non-West (the ethnographic other) to discover those attributes of humanity which are excluded from the West, and thereby achieve a holistic conception of what it means to be human.

In other words, anthropology is "a Western cultural phenomenon generated by the Judeo-Christian cultural structure" (1985:125). This epistemic charter for bifurcating the true from the untrue self, projecting these untrue aspects into some form of other (women, children, primitives, or some deeply hidden, archaic remnant of the past inside the mind), and then going to the other to achieve a unified conception of human existence is a pattern of thinking which may be detected in many other domains of Western culture as well and which is particularly useful in explaining the significance of the symbol of the dream in Western culture.

What is considered outside normal experience, or excluded from the true self, depends on what is considered important in that historical era. The dream may represent the divine, illusion, madness, a feminine weakness, a reservoir of uninhibited memory of childhood, creativity, a distinctive feature of an ethnic group, an archetype, or *doppelganger*. The following chapters explore the role which the dream plays in the manifestation of this cultural system.

I also make use of Pandian's (1990) generalized definition of the shaman. Rather than restrict the term to a part-time religious specialist-healer in technologically primitive societies, he identifies as shamans all religious specialists who have the capacity to commune directly with supernatural beings and powers, in contrast with the priest who propitiates or supplicates supernatural beings and powers in the context of an established social order. The shaman may enter into ecstatic states, undertake mystical journeys to the underworld, battle with gods, and gain knowledge directly from spirit forces through inspiration or possession, whereas a priest officiates at rituals and is the keeper of the sacred knowledge of the society. The shaman is a shaman by virtue of special qualities, the priest by virtue of training. The shaman usually breaks, threatens, or transforms the social order, whereas the priest maintains its social conventions and upholds the moral order. These generalized categories incorporate other religious specialists; for example, prophets, Tantric Buddhists, Baptist healing ministers, and Carl Jung would be classified as shamans.

HISTORICAL PERIODS

The division of the past into historical periods is a cultural act. Such subdivisions as "the Dark Ages," "the Middle Ages," "the Renaissance," and "the Enlightenment" are artificial constructions whose boundaries and definitions indicate the cultural adaptations of the historians who invented them. The Greeks, for example, got their name, *Graeci*, from the Romans; they call themselves *Hellenes* of Hellas. Homer called them *Argives*, *Dannaans*, and *Achaeans* (Finley 1978:18). The following historical periods are referred to in this book:

The Emergence of a Dimly Recognizable
Greece: The Homeric Age

The oral literature of Homer, as well as the Homeric poets, is the inheritance of at least three hundred years of story-telling that followed the destruction of the "Golden Mycenae" of the Achaeans by the Dorians. The Troy described in the great narrative saga of the *Iliad*, written some time between 700 B.C. and 900 B.C., had fallen around 1200 B.C.; the *Odyssey* tells the adventures of a Greek prince from the island of Ithaca who is returning home from Troy. As described by M. I. Finley (1978), the Homeric Age has all the earmarks of later Greek culture: a firmly established family and clan with patriarchal authority, the political institution called the Polis, a taste for the beauty of life and an intense interest in the world (see Hamilton 1964), and distinctive religious and moral outlooks that stressed external evaluations, or as E. R. Dodds (1951) would say, shame as opposed to guilt. The psychology of the Homeric Age reflected a conception of the self as a concrete assemblage of parts rather than a unified whole, or as body vs. soul, or as conscious vs. unconscious.

From about 750 B.C. on, the Greeks expanded their territory beyond the Aegean, but made extensive contacts with the Assyrian Empire and Egypt, and produced economic surpluses that changed the heroic values celebrated by Homer, giving them a more hierarchical, aristocratic standard.

When historians emphasize politico-economic expansion, the period of the sixth to the eighth centuries is referred to as the Age of Expansion and is said to have ended with Greek victory over the Persians in 450 B.C. (a conflict described as valorious by the historian Herodotus and as tragic by the dramatist Aeschylus). During this age, Pindar wrote odes in celebration of the victors of the international athletic festivals that had been established at Olympia, Delphi, and other religious shrines. Looking forward to the intellectual movements for which Greece is most remembered, historians sometimes call this period the Archaic Age, or the early period of the Classical Age.

The Greece of Mythical History: The Classical Age

Although the Age of Expansion produced rational thought in the works of Thales of Miletus, Pythagoras and Empedocles, it was during the Classical Age that Greek rationalism received its greatest impetus in Ionia, particularly in Athens, where rules of rhetoric and skillful argument provided a model for Ciceronian Latin and ultimately the prose of modern English classics of the eighteenth and nineteenth centuries.

The Classical Age of the fifth and fourth centuries B.C. is usually characterized by its art; its attention to regularity, simplicity, and proportion in the balanced composition and the naturalistic rendering of anatomical details, spatial arrangement, and distribution of weight in figures; and its controlled emotion. By the end of the fifth century, historians note a reaction against rationalism. Just as the eighteenth-century Enlightenment was followed by a surge of Romanticism, so the classical emphasis on reason and abstract principles was succeeded by appeals to emotion and individuality. In the face of numerous plagues, thousands visited the healing shrines of Asclepius, and Anaxagoras, Euripides, and Socrates were put on trial for heresy.

The Classical Age was torn by foreign wars and internal revolutions. The conflict between independent states such as Athens and Sparta created a power vacuum which was filled by King Philip of Macedonia, whose son, Alexander the Great, carried Greek culture into the Near East and Asia.

The Decline of Political Greece: The Hellenistic Age, the Roman Empire, and the Age of Anxiety

During the Hellenistic Age that followed the death of Alexander, from the late third century to the triumph of Roman power in Alexandria in the first century B.C., Greek characteristics were modified by "foreign" elements. The classical emphasis on proportion underwent many modifications and sculpture achieved dramatic, emotional, and highly individualized expression. The city of Alexandria in Egypt accumulated an enormous library and supported scholars in their pursuit of medical, mechanical, and mathematical understanding. Greek philosophy continued along rationalist lines of development, elaborating ideas expressed by Plato during the Classical Age. The Stoics, Epicureans, Skeptics, and Cynics all represent various expressions of Greek rationalism.

Hellenistic civilization exerted enormous influence on other peoples, including the Romans who conquered the Greeks almost reluctantly and who approached Greek culture rather like country bumpkins handling a porcelain vase. As Christianity developed, Christian spokesmen wrestled with the nature of their relationship to this "pagan" world view, often resolving their conflict through interpretation of dreams.

The Roman Empire is said to have emerged during the first century B.C.; the precise moment of its end is a subject of great debate. In the second century A.D. an onslaught of barbarian invasions and epidemics brought the Pax Romana to an end and initiated what Dodds (1951) has called the Age of Anxiety. Men turned away from the external world, synthesized Hebraic and Hellenistic inheritances, replaced cyclical with eschatalogical myths, and "pagan intellectuals" took Christianity seriously as indicated either by their attacking it as a serious threat or by developing "apologies" to argue its case (see Glover 1975).   During the second to fourth centuries A.D., the Neoplatonists tried to synthesize classical knowledge with Christianity, and in their encyclopaedic syntheses passed on much of the knowledge of the classical world that was to influence the Middle Ages (e.g., Macrobius's dream classification). In western Europe the Roman Empire disintegrated by the fourth and fifth centuries. Christianity grew stronger and was embraced by Constantine in the fourth century through a dream-based vision. The classical/Judeo-Christian synthesis provided a framework within which European culture emerged during the Middle Ages.

The Emergence of Europe:
The Middle Ages

"Middle Ages" was first used as a term of contempt during the Renaissance to mean the lackluster intermezzo between the Greco-Roman world and the modern world, "modern" referring to Renaissance times. *Media tempestas*, "middle of the storm," appeared in 1469; *media aetas*, "middle age," in 1518; and *medium aevum*, "middle period," in 1604 (Goodrich 1961:v). Ferdinand Lot (1961) attributes the term to Christopher Kellner, a professor of history at the University of Halle, who used it in 1688. Josef Pieper (1960:15-16) quotes Hegel who, in his *Lectures on the History of Philosophy*, skips over the Middle Ages as if it were a sterile ocean, crying "land like a sailor" when he finally gets to Descartes. The term "Dark Ages" is used today, if at all, to refer to the period before 1000 A.D. (the Early Middle Ages), because medieval civilization is now recognized to be a time of important cultural development for Western culture, no longer dim in comparison to the "Renaissance." However, the term "Middle Ages" continues to be used to connote primitive backwardness, especially authoritarian religious fundamentalism; and during the Romantic period medievalism was revived.

When did the "ancient world" end? Politically, it can be said to have ended in the fourth or fifth centuries A.D. with the final phases of disintegration of the Roman Empire (in 395 with the partitioning of the Empire, or in 406 with the attack of the barbarians, or in 476 with the death of Romulus Augustus).

From the ashes of Greco-Roman civilization there rose three new civilizations: Islam, Byzantium, and Western Christendom. In the seventh century, between 630 and 730 A.D., Mohammed united numerous polytheistic tribes and conquered the Byzantine provinces of Syria and Egypt, overwhelmed the Persian empire, and penetrated India, North Africa, and Spain. By the eighth century Islam was a powerful and creative civilization which, having taken control of that "Roman pond," the Mediterranean, precipitated the development of land-locked feudalism in Western Europe (Pirenne 1952).

In the West, European culture was developing as a cultural synthesis of Greco-Roman, Christian and Germanic heritages. Classical culture was preserved by the Christian Church, which at the same time had developed a distinctive philosophical style that both linked it with and separated it from the Greco-Roman period: an emphasis on emotion-based faith over reason, authority over inquiry, and a preoccupation with the truths of divinity as opposed to the phenomenal world.

Warren Hollister (1973) classifies as the Early Middle Ages the period between 500-1050 A.D. when Byzantium, Islam, and Western Christendom rose on ruins of classical Greece and Rome. By about 1050 invasions had stopped and Europe had evolved into a coherent unity. The High Middle

Ages, 1050-1300, are characterized by radical challenges to papal authority. The struggle between the Holy Roman Empire, established in the tenth century, and the Papacy generated debates over the relationship between spiritual and secular matters. The debate over whether papal power was supreme over both spiritual and secular matters was expressed in letter to King John of England in 1214; the Magna Carta was signed in 1215 affirming ancient customs and feudal privileges and supporting the eventual rise of Parliament vs. monarchy. In Italy, Dante's *Divine Comedy*, perhaps the greatest of medieval dream visions, reflected the conflict between papacy and empire. The use of allegory in art and literature, especially the use of the dream vision, played an important role in social change in an era of rigid hierarchy and reverence for tradition.

The High Middle Ages stimulated the expansion of commerce, the rise of towns and an urban middle class, the emergence of universities (see Wieruszowski 1966), and new monastic movements in which many of the ideas of classical-Christian synthesis were debated and developed.

From an economic point of view, the Middle Ages ended in the thirteenth century with the development of towns and modern commercial currents or the suppression of the guilds in 1548. Politically, its ending may be placed in 1453 with the fall of the Eastern Empire, in 1440 with the invention of printing, or in 1492 with the discovery of America.

Defining the Real: The Renaissance

The Middle Ages, if identified with the feudal period, ended in the thirteenth century with the development of towns and modern commercial developments. What is usually given great importance is the change in intellectual atmosphere, which the term Renaissance ("rebirth") implies.

In Italy by the fourteenth century, and during the fifteenth to seventeenth centuries in the rest of Europe, economic expansion, commercial developments, colonial exploration, and the emergence of nation-states contributed to an enthusiasm for worldly life and human endeavor which was reflected in art, literature, science, architecture, and politics. Individual personality was celebrated in biography and realistic art; science benefited, as did alchemy and other occult arts, from an urgent, enthusiastic desire to master the corporeal world. Although such worldly expressions are now interpreted historically as a humanistic reaction against sterile, restrictive medieval asceticism, in fact the Renaissance was as much a religious rebirth as it was a celebration of man and the phenomenal universe. Medieval scholasticism continued in many areas and declined only as universities were secularized after the eighteenth century. Renaissance thinkers sought a unified understanding of the universe and saw all thought and experience as permeated by the divine. Plato, by means of Neoplatonism, with his archetypical Forms and conceptions of divinity, was one of the most widely quoted authors of the Renaissance. In chapter 6 I interpret "Renaissance" as a "Middle Age" between the Middle Ages and the Enlightenment, the latter term denoting commitment to empirical reality.

Defining Mind: The Enlightenment and the Romantic Movement

The Enlightenment and the Age of Reason are both names given to the mainstream of thought in the eighteenth century. To many historians the Enlightenment represents a major demarcation in the emergence of the modern world. Renaissance developments inspired confidence in human reason, encouraged a secular view of the world, and gave rise to various cultural expressions to which the term "Rationalist Movement" has been applied. Dogmatism, intolerance, and censorship were rejected in favor of belief in progress and perfectibility and the study of natural laws.

Having internalized powers hitherto ceded to God, humankind was convinced that it could progress toward perfection on earth. Ignorance could be eliminated with education, the state would serve as the rational instrument of progress, and the Utopian City would become St. Augustine's "City of God," secularized.

The clergy and the nobility, understandably, opposed the loss of authority that trust in natural law conferred on the common man. Strong support for Enlightenment views came from the rising bourgeoisie, whose rebellion against the divine right of kings to rule was expressed in the French Revolution and in the Constitution of the United States of America. History was no longer written to justify a religion or a king, but was imbued with secular detachment (e.g., Gibbon). Social and political criticism flourished in the universities (secularized in the eighteenth century) and in the expanding institution of the coffee house. No longer quivering in the shadow of the stake, Enlightenment thinkers spoke out boldly against dogmatism, censorship, and all forms of restraint and authoritarianism--spiritual, economic, social, and even scientific. Belief in the rational goodness of natural law spawned Adam Smith's laissez-faire economics, Gotthold Lessing's natural religion of morality, Julien Offray de la Mettrie's materialism, Jeremy Bentham's utilitarianism, and Johann Herder's philosophy of cultural nationalism. Materialism permeated philosophy, psychology, and political science. David Hume developed John Locke's theories of learning by sense perception, and Immanuel Kant preserved the soul by creating two sets of standards for knowing.

The extreme rationalism and skepticism of the Enlightenment posed problems for human thought. Trying to think with Hume's method is like trying to walk from *A* to *B* while accepting the fallacy of Zeno's paradox. The Romantic Movement of the late-eighteenth and nineteenth centuries was a philosophical revolt against these problems and against neoclassical ideals, abstract principles and forms, and allegorical representations. Reason and empiricism had promised understanding and social order; instead, it had promoted social unrest, urban blight, child labor in the factories, and widespread anomie. Finding Reason sterile, the Romanticists turned to conscience, emotion, and visions of personal inspiration and tried to remake the world in their own image.

The various literary, artistic, and philosophical movements now lumped together under the phrase "Romantic Movement" promoted a return to nature and belief in the natural goodness of man, as in the writings of Rousseau. They exalted the power of the senses and emotions as opposed to reason and the intellect. Literature of the eighteenth century had experimented with non-linear structure and syntactical discontinuities, suggesting that an unpredictable realm lay beyond rational waking consciousness. Romantic writers and artists pursued this theme, emphasizing involuntary and unconscious mental forces. Long before Sigmund Freud, there emerged a layer-cake model of the psyche: rational over irrational, adult over infantile. The truth, having been relegated to reason (man's traditional link with the divine in Western culture), was now being excavated in the Unconscious. The dream, which Freud used in a grand cultural synthesis, provided a new ladder to the gods, and a strategy for healing civilization. Freud's use of the dream provided a cultural solution to a Western dilemma.

The Twentieth-Century Synthesis

The twentieth century is a time of rapid technological change, widespread industrialization and urbanization, and a growing awareness of the need to synthesize a global culture. Just as Freud may be interpreted as the person who integrated the untrue self with the true self (as conceptualized in the architecture of the mind), so anthropology is playing a similar role today (or since the Renaissance) with regard to the ethnographic other.

One of the most important changes to have occurred in the late nineteenth and twentieth centuries was the emergence of a new epistemology. Rooted in John Locke's *tabula rasa*, which was initially proposed by Aristotle, the idea that our categories of knowing depend upon society was most clearly developed by Emile Durkheim, who expanded the ideas of William Robertson Smith. The awareness that we structure the world according to culturally based categories of understanding is widespread in the disciplines, but it is explicitly developed and applied in a cross-cultural context by anthropologists. I explore the usefulness of this perspective in the final chapter.

2

From *Oneiros* to *Daimon:* The Interiorization of the Sacred Other in Greek Conceptions of the Dream

"Nothing moves in the world," it has been said, "which is not Greek in origin."

C. E. Robinson, *Greek Psychology*

European thinking begins with the Greeks. They have made it what it is: our only way of thinking; its authority, in the Western world, is undisputed.

Bruno Snell, *The Discovery of the Mind*

The Greeks, who gave to mankind its most imaginative myths, have themselves become almost mythical.

C. M. Bowra, *The Greek Experience*

GREECE AND THE FOUNDATIONS OF WESTERN IDEAS AND CONCEPTS

Discussions of most Western ideas and concepts inevitably refer to Greece; indeed, the Greek intellectual tradition often serves as an important symbol of Western ethnicity. But as Michael Herzfeld (1987:7) points out, Greece constitutes a paradox. The cradle from which "we" emerged and ancestral to "us," Greece is nevertheless removed from us through mythic time and occupies a different cultural space. It is "not us" although we claim it as "our own." From the Homeric Age to the Classical Age, the semantics, pragmatics, and syntactics of the dream shift from very unfamiliar patterns to patterns that hover on the verge of the recognizable.

HOMER'S VISITING DREAMS

If it is true that European history began with the Greeks, it is equally true that Greek history began with the world of Odysseus.
                                   M. I. Finley, *The World of Odysseus*

As stated by Finley (1978:123), the Homeric world "was unable to visualize any achievement or relationship except in concrete terms. The gods were anthropomorphized, the emotions and feelings were located in specific organs of the body, even the soul was materialized." The conceptions of the dream in Homeric Greece (ca. eighth century B.C.) reflect this same tendency to personify and externalize aspects of experience. The dream was not conceived of as an internal experience, a state of mind, or a message from the irrational unconscious to the conscious ego. Rather, it was an objectified messenger, a supernatural agent sent by a deity (Zeus in the *Iliad*, Athena in the *Odyssey*), or in some cases by the dead, for example, the appearance of Patroclus to Achilles in Book 23 of the *Iliad*. One did not "have" a dream; one "saw" a dream figure *(oneiros)*. The dream figure usually came through a keyhole, stood at the sleeper's head, told the dreamer that he or she was asleep, and delivered a message (see Messer 1918). In Book 2 of the *Iliad*, Zeus uses a dream to fool Agamemnon:

> Zeus could not sleep. For he was pondering how he could destroy crowds of men on the battlefield and cover Achilles with glory. It seemed to be the best plan to send a bad dream to King Agamemnon. So he called one, and spoke plainly and to the point: "Away, Bad Dream! Go to the Achaian camp; enter the hut of King Agamemnon, and tell him exactly what I say. Bid him arm the Achaians with all haste; for now he may take the city of Troy. The Olympians are no longer divided; Hera has now bent them all by her entreaties, and troubles hang over the Trojans." Away went the Dream; quickly he flew to the camp . . . .The Dream leaned over his head in the shape of Nestor Neleides, whom Agamemnon respected most of all the elders, and spoke in these words: "You are asleep, O son of Atreus, the lord of many horses!. . . I am a messenger from Zeus, who far away cares for you and pities you." Then the Dream departed. . . . The King awoke with the divine voice echoing about him. (Rouse 1938:3-24)

In Book 4 of the *Odyssey*, Athena sends a dream to console Penelope:

She made a phantom, and fashioned it after the likeness of a woman, Iphthime. . . . And she sent it to the house of divine Odysseus to bid Penelope. . . to cease from her weeping and tearful lamentation. So the phantom passed into the chamber by the thong of the bolt, and stood above her head and spake unto her. (Butcher and Lang 1909:69-70)

TRUE AND FALSE DREAMS

The Homeric writings contain several devices for distinguishing between true and false dreams. In some cases the deity sending the dream is described as purposefully sending false information, such as Zeus who sought to deceive Agamemnon in Book 2 of the *Iliad*. The distinction between the gates of horn and ivory through which true and false dreams come was made in Book 19 of the *Odyssey*, and although it constitutes a relatively minor reference in the Homeric writings, it was taken up by numerous writers and is still being used today (for example, Highbarger 1940; Hill 1967). Penelope, in a conversation with the disguised Odysseus, says:

Stranger, verily dreams are hard, and hard to be discerned; nor are all things therein fulfilled for men. Twain are the gates of shadowy dreams, the one is fashioned of horn and one of ivory. Such dreams as pass through the portals of sawn ivory are deceitful, and bear tidings that are unfulfilled. But the dreams that come forth through the gates of polished horn bring a true issue, whosoever of mortals beholds them. (Butcher and Lang 1909:282)

The image of the two gates crops up in Plato (*Charmides*), Horace (*Odes*), Virgil (*Aeneid*), Statius (*Silvae*), Lucian (*A True Story*; *Somnium*), and elsewhere (see Highbarger 1940). The device is useful; not all dreams were perceived to be significant predictors of future events. Later writers distinguished between oracular, visionary dreams and those that reflected bodily discomfort or wish fulfillment. The image of horn and ivory gates was an externalized representation of the perceived difference between true and false dreams and served as a powerful metaphor despite the fact that it probably originated from a play on words (see Messer 1918:35).

HESIOD'S DREAM FAMILY

In contrast with the Homeric tradition, the Hesiodic tradition, also of the eighth century B.C., gives dreams a more elaborate heritage and geography. Dreams are chthonic, the children of Night who live with their siblings, Fate,

Death, and Sleep under the earth in a windswept cave called Tartarus (see West 1966, especially lines 713-766 of *Theogony*).

INCUBATION

In the process of incubation (sleeping in a holy place), sleepers actively sought contact with divine beings or their messengers. Incubation had been practiced by the Egyptians and Babylonians long before the cult of Asclepius became popular in the fifth century. Divine beings such as Phobetor, the Terrifier, took human or animal shape in dreams and provided predictions of the future. Incubation in Greece appears to have been associated with pre-Hellenic cults of the Earth, and Asclepius was initially worshipped as an earth-spirit with the serpent as his symbol. In the fifth century, Asclepius was elevated to the status of a god and associated with Apollo. The cult of Asclepius persisted in Rome after the decline of Greece, and medical incubation is still practiced among some Greek rural populations   (see Hamilton 1906; Edelstein and Edelstein 1945).

THE HOME OF DREAMS

Humans, gods, and dream messengers all had their natural and necessary loci and functions. Certain figures emerged as bridges between the human world and the realm of the supernatural, such as Asclepius himself, Mercury the messenger, and Hermes. They bring messages from the supernatural or in some cases conduct souls (in forms not very recognizable to us today) back to the realm of the supernatural. In the *Odyssey* (xxiv, 1-18), for example, Hermes leads the gibbering, bat-like wraiths (the breath-soul which leaves the body at death or unconsciousness) to the gates of death's kingdom, just outside of which is the Land of Dreams. In Book 23 of the *Iliad*, the shade of Patroclus visits Achilles while he sleeps and asks him to bury him so that he may pass the gates of Hades instead of wandering aimlessly outside the gates. When Achilles reaches out to him, the soul vanishes "like smoke," making a sound variously translated as "twittering" or "gibbering," a term also used, according to William Messer (1918:16), for the sounds of birds and the cracking made by wrestlers' backs. Hermes provides an interesting linkage between the celestial Olympians of Homer and the chthonic underworld realms of Hesiod, for his father is Zeus and his mother is Maia, and he was conceived in the middle of the night and born in a cave (*Homeric Hymn to Hermes*, 1-23).

In Ovid (*Metamorphoses*), Dreams become the sons rather than the brothers of Sleep, and Sleep's palace is located near the Cimmerians, who, in the Odyssey, live at "the limits of the world" at the border of the "deep flowing Oceanus" near the palace of Hades;   the land and city of the

Cimmerians is "shrouded in mist and cloud, and never does the shining sun look down on them with his rays . . . but deadly night is outspread over miserable mortals" (Butcher and Lang 1909:162). Lucian (*A True Story*) substitutes state for family, changing Dreams from siblings or sons to citizens of the Isle of Dreams, whose ruler is Sleep.

HOMERIC PSYCHOLOGY

Understanding how the Homeric Greeks conceived the nature of the body, mind, self, and soul sheds light on the meaning and uses of the dream during this time. In the Homeric period, embedded in a tightly knit social network, humans acted out the expectations of their fellows; they had no will and thus no guilt, but only the capacity for shame. The gods, in their parallel world, extended these social manipulations and moved men around like puppets, sending them *ate* (divine temptation), *menos* (vital energy), and divine messages in the form of *oneiros* (dream messengers). They were not judges of good or evil but acted out the range of deceit and loyalty which mirrored the human world, taking favorites in their own battles and establishing a mythological charter for the complexity of human behavior. If a human suffered from the actions of these external agents, it was a source of misfortune, but not guilt. The cause was external; sin needs will and is a reflection of the existence of an inner consciousness that can choose between good and evil, between the true and the untrue self.

According to Snell (1960), Homeric writings express a different conception of body, mind, intellect, and self than the more familiar unified conceptions that were to exist later. The "body" was not a unit but an aggregate or assemblage of parts: one had "limbs," not even whole arms, legs, and a trunk but "hands, lower arms, upper arms, feet, calves, and thighs" Snell 1960:310); "skin" (*chros*, as in the outer limit of the body); *demas* (the structure or frame); and *soma* referred to a corpse. "Not until the classical art of the fifth century do we find attempts to depict the body as an organic unit whose parts are mutually correlated. In the preceding period the body is a mere construct of independent parts variously put together" (Snell 1960:6).

Just as there is no single word for the body, the Homeric writings lack a single word that describes the mind or soul in contrast with the body. An individual is an assemblage of mental forces, just as he is an assemblage of physical parts. People do not "make up their minds" to act; they are moved by external forces which impinge on their separate organs.

The word *psyche* appears in Homeric writings, but refers to the quality of life that is an attribute of the physical aggregate (the breath or air that leaves the body at death, through the mouth, and flutters off, bat-like, to Hades). It is a "semi-concrete organ" (Snell 1960:9) that remains within the bounds set for the physical organs. In the *Iliad*, a man is alive "as long as my breath remains in my breast and my knees are in motion" (10.89, translated by Snell 1960:9). In contrast, the term *psyche* as used by Heraclitus in the sixth and fifth century B.C. reached into infinity; it transcended the limitations of the material body. In the emerging dualistic contrast between mind and body, *psyche* was gradually identified with the mind, or the principle of cognition. Plato in particular helped to crystallize this dualistic conception of the physical body tied to the world of appearances and the mind or soul that because of its capacity for reason, can transcend the temporal, decaying realm of the body and participate in the timeless, eternal world of divine reason.

During the Homeric age there was no such thing as an unconscious. Knowledge was what was known, relatively clear or unclear, and was a function of the organ of perception (*noos*). What a person did not "know" was sent by the gods. The gods might send misleading dreams, such as the deceitful visitor ("false vision" or "bad dream") sent to Agamemnon by Zeus in the *Iliad*; or in the *Odyssey* falseness depended on whether the dream messenger issued from the gate of horn or that of ivory.

Anything strange or unexpected or abnormal was caused by external agents (the gods or fate); it had nothing to do with misconduct, for which a dreamer should feel guilty. The dream was not part of a bridge to the self but part of the not-known, outside of the self. A person might feel misfortune or a sense of shame, but not guilt or a sense of sin. A sense of sin needs an awareness of some part of the self which is untrue. Even the "ego" of the Homeric Greeks was not the twentieth century ego; it was composed of many disconnected parts conversing with each other. Besides *psyche*, a person had *thymos*, an organ of motion, emotion, or agitation that imparts movement to limbs, is the locus of joy, anger, and other emotions; and *noos*, an organ of reflection, thought, or clear images. There was no unified self that could be validated by a religious charter for the true self. If one's *thymos* experienced greater pain, or one's *noos* had greater insight, the source was external, some gift or gesture of the gods.

During the Homeric Age, and continuing on into the Classical Age, the self was a loosely assembled set of parts whose various impulses and characteristics were considered part of the natural scheme of things. The dream was an objective messenger whose tidings--true, false, predictive, misleading--were, like the complex and contradictory behavior of the gods, a reflection of the natural order of human life.

SHAMANISM AND MIND-BODY DUALISM

During the seventh century, the Greeks were introduced to different kinds of shamanistic rituals and beliefs as a result of trade and colonization of the Black Sea. Dodds (1951) suggests that incorporation of such beliefs is responsible for the emergence of a new concept of body and soul that appears at the end of the Archaic Age. We find at this time a new version of the dream that was linked with a new psychology: a conception of divinity within humans themselves. *Psyche* is no longer the breath-soul, the principle of life on the ordinary empirical level, but an occult entity, the indestructible and timeless part of the self. During the Classical Age, the self became a unified orderly personality whose "true" element was reason linked with the divine. *Psyche*, previously only one of many personified attributes of experience, became the soul and the source of divinity within man. According to Pindar and Xenophon, the *psyche* takes on its divine character, its ability to predict the future, its ability to *know*, when the body is asleep. As expressed by Cicero in *De Divinatione* (I, li, 115), the soul is liberated from the body, from the constraints of time and space, during sleep. The body limits the ability of the soul to know. According to Plato, the rational soul can predict the future (true forms, part of the orderly nature of the universe) once the hubbub of the senses dies down.

Pindar signifies the emergence of a new culture pattern based on shamanism imported to Greece from the north (Dodds 1951: chapter 5) consisting of the "puritanical" idea that the soul, which is a fragment of divinity, is imprisoned in the body. Pindar's famous passage, used to date the emergence of this new concept of a divine soul whose metaphysical destiny opposed it to the limits of the body, is as follows:

> while the body of all men is subject to over-mastering death, an image of life remaineth alive, for it alone cometh from the gods. But it sleepeth, while the limbs are active; yet, to them that sleep, in many a dream it giveth presage of things delightful or doleful. (Fragment 131; also see Jaeger 1947)

In this new culture pattern, the soul is perceived as older than the body, and as having the capacity to understand things more clearly. In other words, human identity now has two elements, one true and the other false. The false identity is rooted in the impure, dross-filled, decaying body. Orphic and Pythagorean cults emphasized purificatory rituals (*catharsis*) and food taboos (such as not eating beans because flatulence would disturb the soul's calm) that minimized the influence of the body on the ability of the soul to know Truth. The body was not the real self; each individual was responsible for the purity of one's soul, which made possible cycles of reincarnation and transmigration of the soul.

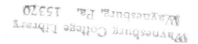

PLATO'S CONCEPT OF THE SOUL

By the fifth century, these ideas were well established. Plato gave full philosophical treatment to the concept of a soul distinct from the body, as the seat of intellect and personality whose ability to transcend the dross of the phenomenal world depends on the individual's moral conduct (following the path of the true self). In the *Apology* (29D4 ff. and 30A7 ff.), Socrates stresses the importance of taking care of the soul, and in *Crito* (47E-48A) asks, "do we believe that this part of us, whatever it may be, in which right and wrong operate, is of less importance than the body?" *Charmides* states (156D ff.): "all good and evil . . . originates . . . in the soul, and overflows from thence, as if from the head into the eyes. And therefore if the head and body are to be well, you must begin by curing the soul--that is the first and essential thing."

In Plato's writings, knowledge is something independent of the body, and its realization depends on the soul being able to extract itself from the influences of the body; turning away from the body leads toward, not away from truth. At the end of the *Republic*, Plato describes, in the myth of Er, the process by which each soul, before it goes on to a new body, drinks from the River of Forgetfulness. Wise souls drink less and thus remember more of Truth. Knowledge is the process by which the soul recovers what it has always known but is obscured from knowing because of the influence of the body. From *Meno* and *Phaedo* on, the soul is portrayed as dominant over the body, as the true self by virtue of its divinity, and the body is a mere temporary and occluding shell.

As T. M. Robinson (1970) points out, Plato's concept of the soul is complex. It is often equated with the self (*Charmides, Protagoras* 313AI-C3, *Phaedo* 115c, and *Republic* 469D6-9), but may also be spoken of as if it were subdivided. For example, in the wise man who has cultivated his reason and tamed his passions, the appetitive part of the soul sleeps with the body whereas the rational part of the soul, in isolated purity, is able to understand the unknown past, present, and future (*Republic* 572a); or the liver is perceived as capable of divination, and reason interprets the images at the surface of the liver (*Timaeus* 70e-72b); or there is a part of the soul "which resembles God; and he who looks at this and at the whole class of things divine, at God and at wisdom, will be most likely to know himself." (*Timaeus* 133CI-6) By the *Republic*, the importance of reason is clearly evident. The *Phaedo* contains the most well developed statement of Plato's "Theory of Ideas" and the immortality of the soul. In his discussion of suicide, Socrates distinguishes between body and soul as independent substances. To know reality, the soul must have a minimum of contact with the body (65C8-9); bodily sensation interferes with the powers of cognition by which it comes to know "reality." The soul is the true self, the body its untrue, misleading, tempting non-self.

In examining the thesis of a tripartite soul in Plato's writings, Robinson concludes that the soul is very much a unity; the soul is the self, the self is the intellect, and the soul-self is contrasted with the body, from which stem desires. But there is some discussion in *Gorgias* (503E ff.) of "elements" of the soul, or in the *Republic*, the soul is referred to as having three parts or principles (ratiocinative, spirited, desiderative; reason, impulse, and harmonious judgment or balance)--implying the possibility of some inner conflict or disease of the soul, health being a by-product of balance or harmony. The soul is unified but at the same time has separate desires that must be attuned and kept in balance. The soul can be corrupted by injustice, licentiousness, cowardice, and ignorance (609A8-BI, 609BII-CI, 609D4 ff.). The soul should be purified; the soul is marred by communion with the body. It can only fully realize itself when it is no longer in contact with the body. A soul bound to the body is untrue to its genuine nature, to reality. The *Republic* (435E ff.) admits that conflict within the soul is possible, but the philosopher can achieve the next best synthesis to death (in death lies full freedom of the soul):

> The soul is most like that which is divine, immortal, intelligible, uniform, indissoluble, and ever self-consistent and invariable, whereas body is most like that which is human, mortal, multiform, unintelligible, dissoluble, and never self-consistent. (*Phaedo* 79D9-80CI)

DREAMS AND THE SOUL IN THE CLASSICAL AGE

We are left, then, during the Classical Age, with the image of an enduring, true self-soul in contrast with the body, whose wisdom is eternal, whose knowledge is a given, and the knowing of it is a matter of learning the principles by which one may philosophically separate oneself from the negative influences of the body.

Dreams, in this context, are a form of higher knowledge. A temperate man who has cultivated his reason is more likely to have dreams in which he apprehends truth (*Republic*, 752a); the rational part of the soul, if the appetitive part is quiet, can comprehend unknown things of the past, present, and future in dreams. In *Timaeus*, Plato attributes divinatory dreaming to the liver rather than to reason; but reason needs to interpret it once the person wakes up. Even Aristotle, who later denied divination through dreams (in *On Dreams* and *On Divination in Sleep*, Aristotle specifies that dreams are predictive only insofar as symptoms ignored during waking crop up during sleep, and insofar as they suggest a means by which the dreamer may fulfill a wish), seems to endorse the idea in a few early fragments that when the soul is isolated in sleep it assumes its "true nature" and can foresee the future.

Dodds's thesis about the influence of shamanism on Greek culture must be understood in its own historical context, and will be examined again in chapter 7. Dodds wrote *The Greeks and the Irrational* (1951) in response to the Romantic emphasis on primitive art and feeling which devalued the Greek contribution, which was conceived as primarily rational. In the process of affirming the Greek capacity for irrationality, Dodds reiterates the Western polarization of rationality and irrationality, legitimizing the irrational as a mode of strengthening the rational. In his concluding statements he draws a parallel with modern times and says that we will succeed, where the Greeks failed, in retaining rationalism and an open society. We will succeed, he says, because we are aware of the power and process of the irrational, as reflected by the development of psychoanalytic modes of understanding the world.

The Otherness that the dream represents in the romantic, psychoanalytic mode of the nineteenth and twentieth centuries is not yet present in Western culture; but the bifurcation of the self had begun and was taken up in full force by the Judeo-Christian tradition. Empedocles refers to the occult self not as *psyche*, the vital warmth associated with the body that is reabsorbed into the fiery aether when the body dies, but as *daimon*, "the carrier of man's potential divinity and actual guilt" (Dodds 1951:153), the occult self that persists through reincarnation. The *daimon* suffers in the prison of the body and quests for the eternal reality of which it is a small, divine fragment; and it is this *daimon*, this occult, interiorized other, that will shift in meaning, use, and relationship to other ideas during the next two millennia.

3

True and False Dreams in the Judeo-Christian Tradition: Neoplatonist Dream Theories and Biblical Dreams

In Homeric times, dreams were external to humans and were personified as supernatural visitors. Whether they were true or false depended on the intent of the supernatural being who sent them (for example, the bad, deceptive dream that was sent to mislead Agamemnon) or on whether the dreams are sent via the gates of horn or ivory.

By the Classical Age dreams had become interiorized and were symptoms of the communion between the occult self and the divine. True dreams occurred when the body slept and the soul could wander at will, free from earthly shackles; false dreams reflected the appetites and discomforts of the body. The "self" was bifurcated into the divine, occult self linked to the timeless, eternal realm of Ideas and ultimate Good, and the limiting, shadowy, insubstantial body tied to the world of appearances.

With the development and intellectual dominance of the Judeo-Christian tradition in Western culture, true and false dreams came to mean something different: The divine itself was bifurcated into good and evil. Angels and devils populated the eternal realm, fighting for the occult soul. Dreams were still a bridge to the supernatural, but dreamers were encouraged to distrust their dreams, not knowing if they were sent by angels or devils. Dreams were more than a bridge to the supernatural; they were vehicles of persuasion in the battle between good and evil for the dreamer's soul.

THE DAIMONIC IN THE JUDEO-CHRISTIAN TRADITION

In Plato's *Symposium*, the *daimonic* is that which is intermediate between God and mortal; God has no contact with humans except through the daimonic, especially in dreams during sleep. In *Timaeus*, Plato refers to the unitary soul as the *daimon*, and this appears to be more like the concept of a spirit than a rational soul. Passages in Laws imply that the heavenly daimon has an evil daimonic counterpart, a hereditary root of wickedness conceived of as man's "Titan nature," after a myth about the Titans. Drawing on that concept, Joseph Kraft stated in the *Los Angeles Times* (8 August 1984) that "inside most Americans, especially most successful Americans, there is a little bit of Nixon. It is the bad angel in the national psyche." As Dodds points out (1965:37), the use of terms such as *daimon* and *daimonios* was a novelty in Plato's day. But, by the second century daimons, angels, aeons, or spirits were generally recognized as mediators between humans and God, and dreams were an accepted medium of communication. A daimonic personality was a spirit medium, a spokesman for the supernatural: a shaman. If the supernatural communication were believed, the medium was said to be a prophet; if disbelieved, a "demon-ridden" "belly-talker" (Dodds 1965:53). Christians eventually distinguished between true and false prophets (those possessed by pneuma or spirit, and those possessed by demons); pagan gods were believed to exist, but were demons or fallen gods.

The use of the term Judeo-Christian is relatively recent and first appears in the 1899 *Literary Guide* (Silk 1984:65) to refer to historical connections between Judaism and Christianity. During the twentieth century it has come to mean values and beliefs shared in common as an intrinsic part of the Western tradition of the post-Roman period. Judeo-Christian values are sometimes identified as a cultural system that protests anti-Semitic fascism and Communism and that promotes "world-redemption and the progressive unfolding of the world-spirit" (Morgenstern quoted in Silk 1984:68).

ESCHATOLOGY AND DUALISM

Christianity is a synthesis of Hellenistic and Hebraic elements; but according to theologians such as Reinhold Niebuhr (1955), the Hebraic influence made the more significant contribution to the definition of humankind and the relationship of human history to the divine. The Hellenistic equation of the self with mind and the belief that history is rational were less significant than the Hebraic emphasis on a personal God playing a role in a particular group's historical existence, the conception of an exclusive God who has a special covenant with a particular community. Christianity is an eschatological religion, meaning it has a final end in view. Dreams have the potential in Western culture to enable God to act through humans toward that end. David Miller (1970) suggests that Freud's recollection of past history to achieve meaning for the present and Jung's vision of completeness achieved through dream images that unify and transform present, conscious experience both reflect this eschatological vision of Western theology. The dream continues to play an important role in an ongoing cultural system.

In the early sixth century B.C., Zeno argued that the world was static and timeless; that there was but one Being, "timeless, changeless, a superatom or moad of existence--divine without being godlike. . . . Such as the ultimate nature of reality" (Schneer 1969:15). When the Classical Greek philosophers took up the debate on the nature of reality, they sought the fundamental ingredients of which the cosmos was made, and the laws by which these ingredients took on various expressions in the changing, circular flux of order and chaos. The cosmos was permeated by mind. Nature was a thinking world; to "know" reality was to comprehend the nature of its order. The laws that generated diversity were mathematical; they could be known through the exercise of reason. To know such ideas became, for Plato, the goal of the philosopher trying to understand the nature of existence. The ideas lying behind phenomena were more important than the phenomena themselves. Mathematics was "queen" of the sciences, a "pure" science undiluted by the decaying, changing dregs of the material world which she wore as a cloak of expression.

From the world of timeless, static Being, a living Cosmos throbbing with the expression of mathematical laws and geometric form, there emerged a separation between Idea and the material world and between the mind of humankind that could grasp these eternal ideas and the decaying body in which the mind was housed. The mind-body, spirit-matter dualism was to play an increasingly central role in Western culture as it was grafted onto the Hebraic emphasis on the role of the divine in a lineal model of history.

The Hebraic tradition took the mythology of natural cycles that characterized the ancient Near East and historicized it (Wilder 1970:87), turning human history into a lineal progression toward a final end. God gave birth to his chosen people, people who represented "health and truth and light, integrity and the prospect of perfection" (Campbell 1970:40) and would eventually be victorious over the rest of the world as God fulfilled his covenant to establish "a supernaturally endowed society" (Campbell 1970: 139). Christianity universalized the concept of the chosen people but retained the Hebraic eschatological vision.

Mircea Eliade (1959) and others have contrasted religious systems incorporating such Final Judgments with cyclical, preservative religions that provide eternal continuity. In Hinduism, for example, creation is not the act of a single god; the universe has existed forever, waxing and waning in cycles, much as in Zeno's conception of a divine, timeless superatom of being. Each human is *brahman*; and as such, each human is not required to examine his thoughts and behavior for signs that he is or is not one of the chosen or saved. Eden is not some divine paradise, once lost but finally to be regained when the last trumpet sounds, but "the garden of one's soul" (Campbell 1970:157). In the Judeo-Christian Bible, one's ultimate loyalty is to God, not man, as Campbell (1970:164) paraphrases Matthew 6:19-21: "what ills this terrestrial life has wrought, where moth and rust consume and thieves break in and steal. Let us lay up our treasure in heaven--or in extinction." But to the Hindus and Greeks, god is existence; and it is human existence that deserves one's sympathy.

History is irrelevant in Eastern religions. The irrelevance of history pertains even to the interpretation of dreaming, which in the *Upanishads* (Hindu texts that deal with the nature of reality) is related not to the unique history of an individual, serving to express his conflicts or fulfill his desires, but in its position in a continuum of existence, as one phase of a vast spectrum of consciousness that extends from ordinary waking consciousness to the being of inanimate objects (Barfield 1970).

With the breakdown of the Hellenistic world, the decline of the Roman Empire, and the general decay that produced an "Age of Anxiety" (Dodds 1965), Christian eschatology strengthened communities and focused their attention on the Apocalypse. The end would come, and one must be allied with the powers of good, cast out devils, and separate oneself from the evils of the phenomenal world, for the true treasures are in heaven. Christians were intolerant of other beliefs, met in secret societies, advocated the end of the Roman Empire and its replacement by a Christian god on earth, and were reviled by educated "pagans" as a religion of blind faith (*pistis*, the lowest grade of cognition) appealing to the uneducated masses. Whereas the educated pagans such as Lucian, Galen, and Marcus Aurelius were astonished by the willingness of Christians to die for unproved assertations, St. Paul represented *pistis* as the foundation of Christian life. The emphasis on blind faith and revelation of God's will contributed to one pattern in the Christian use of dreams that waxed and waned, along with the more classical emphasis on reason, up through modern times.

Although the early Christian churches varied greatly in their interpretation of the relationship between the divine and human history, some seeing God as an impersonal greatness too vast and self-contained to have any interest in significant humanity, by the fourth century the divine was intimately linked with the self. Human history was the unfolding of the divine will; and dreams served as a bridge to understand the divine. Through the Bible, they were a form of divination; in the allegorical literary forms which served as teaching devices during the high Middle Ages they provided a vehicle by which all forms of knowing and knowledge could be expressed; and in individual lives, they were significant as a manifestation and disclosure of good or evil, as God's presence (or Satan's) in a personal historical context.

The Greeks conceived of the material world as placing constraints on the freedom of the soul, as in Plotinus, who said that life is God's play, staged with human puppets who are but eternal shadows of the inner man; action is an inferior shadow of contemplation. But, no Stoic, Aristotelian, or Platonist condemned the cosmos as a whole. This was a product of radical dualism, of Christian Gnosticism and related ideas. Gnosticism was a dualistic religious and philosophical movement of the late Hellenistic and early Christian eras which had numerous sects by the second century A.D. It promised salvation through occult knowledge, and may be traced back to the Jewish kabbalah, Hellenistic mystery cults, Iranian religious dualism (Zoroastrianism), and Babylonian and Egyptian mythology. Christian ideas were quickly incorporated.

Gnosticism taught that the world is ruled by evil archons, among them the deity of the Old Testament, who hold the spirit of man captive. Christ was an intermediary eternal being, or *aeon*, sent to restore the lost knowledge of man's divine origin, and in learning secret formulae gnostics will be free from the evil archons at death and will be restored to their heavenly abode.

The theory of a malevolent creator was part of a wave of pessimism sweeping over the West. The Devil entered the West by means of late Judaism, which transformed Satan from God's agent into God's adversary, and St. Paul took him over and made him "god of this world" (see Dodds 1965). By the fourth century A.D., the pagan demons that had been both bad and good had become totally evil (Le Goff 1988:212).

St. Augustine, whose influence on Christianity was second only to that of St. Paul, presented the Christian view of history in *The City of God* (A.D. 412). History was God's preparation of two mystical cities, one of God and one of the Devil. Humankind, said Augustine, will eventually belong to one or the other. Corrupt and helpless, humans require God's grace to achieve salvation; history will demonstrate God's will. The struggle between good and evil is the basic fact of history, more significant than the struggle of armies and empires. Faith, like the philosophical gold of the alchemists, could achieve psychic transformation. And as Jacques Le Goff suggests (1988:16), during the Middle Ages "the dream was one of the primary battlegrounds on which God contended with the Devil for the possession of man's soul."

Individuals gathered what data they could, including the messages provided by dreams, to see what role they played in God's plan, in the great battle to win through to the City of God. Each individual had only one life; he had no second chance through reincarnation (although eventually he had some chance after death through the deeds that the living could perform to get the beloved dead person out of Purgatory; see Le Goff 1984). At the end of that life he must weigh his soul on the eternal scales and give good weight. Throughout that life he inspected his actions, thoughts, and dreams for signs of the untrue, rejected characteristics of the divinely sanctioned self; and he used examples of heresy and evil to define the true self. The existence of nightmares and troubled sleep became proof of the eternal battle of the soul with demons.

SHAMANIC ECSTASY VERSUS
ALLEGORICAL DREAM VISIONS

During the Middle Ages, two patterns in the use of dreams may be distinguished: a shamanic quest for direct contact by individuals with the supernatural through ecstatic states and the use of the dream vision as moralizing allegories, fabulous narratives used by an established Church to teach its understanding of the universe and to reinforce its hierarchy. The first was typical in the early days of the Middle Ages, and continued as a form of dream autobiography, especially among the clergy, from monks to saints, who wrestled with demons in their personal quest for salvation. The second reached its apex with the *Romance of the Rose* of the thirteenth century, Dante's *Divine Comedy* of the fourteenth, and various tales of *Everyman* that became popular during the fifteenth century.

For an understanding of the categories of the dream by which these genres may be distinguished, it is important to look at the Neoplatonists who formed a bridge between the classical world and the Middle Ages, in particular the writings of Macrobius. This chapter will include a discussion of the dream theories and classifications of the Neoplatonists and how they related to the interpretation of dreams during the establishment of Christianity. The next chapter will review the allegory of the dream vision that was such an important literary device in the late Middle Ages.

INTEGRATING CLASSICAL AND CHRISTIAN
INTERPRETATIONS IN THE SECOND TO
FOURTH CENTURIES A.D.

Toward the end of the second century, pagan intellectuals began to take Christianity seriously and to perceive Christians as a menace to the social order. They did not burn incense on the Emperor's birthday, they refused to serve in the Roman army against the barbarians, and they advocated replacement of the Roman Empire with a Christian God on earth (see Dodds 1965). Celsus published *The True Teachings* in A.D. 178 to check the spread of Christianity; he warned parents that Christians encouraged their children to disobey their fathers and schoolmasters. Pagan slaves denounced their Christian masters, and both Christians and Jews were tortured for evidence of blasphemous behavior (such as incest and cannibalism) during their secret meetings.

In the third century A.D. Christians were alternately left alone and persecuted. While Christians were being blamed for earthquakes in Asia Minor, epidemics in Rome, and droughts everywhere, some Roman emperors added Abraham and Christ to the pantheon of their temples, and Christian writers such as Clement of Alexandria encouraged the assimilation of Greek knowledge so that Christianity would not just be a religion for the uneducated.   In A.D. 248 Origen wrote *Contra Celsus* in defense of Christianity. He interpreted the New Testament by means of the allegorical method (reading the text for numerous levels of truth) and anticipated St. Augustine's three levels of vision, so important to an understanding of medieval epistemology, by specifying literal, moral, and mystical ways of knowing.   Origen studied under the pagan philosopher Ammonius Saccas, who later was the teacher of Plotinus (see following section).

By the end of the third century Christianity had still not made much of an impression on the aristocracy, but that changed when Constantine converted in the early fourth century. Constantine, ruler of Gaul and Britain, invaded Italy to seize the Western imperial throne. Before the Battle of Milvian Bridge in A.D. 312, Constantine is said by Lactantius to have had a day vision in which a flaming cross appeared in the sky inscribed with the words, "By this sign thou shalt conquer," and in the night Christ came to him in a dream and told him to adopt the cross as his banner (see Dodds 1965; Hollister 1973; Le Goff 1988:219). He won the battle, and in the following year issued the edict of Milan in which Christianity was recognized. In 394 Christianity (and dreams) were validated in another victorious battle, this one fought by Theodosius I, Emperor of Rome, at the river Frigidas; at sunset he had a dream in which John the Baptist and the apostle Philip appeared to him and encouraged him to fight on (see Le Goff 1988:219; Hill 1967:9). In A.D. 496 the Frankish conqueror Clovis converted to Christianity when his own pagan gods did nothing to help him during a battle. (The bad Latin used by Bishop Gregory of Tours to write the history of the Franks in the sixth century testifies to the breakdown of classical culture, but he respected the classics; for example, he considered the Latin writer Capella's curriculum to be the highest example of human wisdom.) Under these conditions of state acceptance, Christian scholarship and theology reached full maturity.   Pagan scholarship was an integral part of this development, especially in the writings of the Neoplatonists.

The Neoplatonists

The Neoplatonists were a small group of compilers who, as the Roman Empire declined, sought to preserve classical civilization. They usually began as pagans but died Christians, and helped to transmit knowledge of classical philosophy, liberal arts and sciences to the medieval world. Neoplatonism itself dates from the writings of Plotinus in the mid-third century. Plotinus was a Roman philosopher who, in the interest of studying the philosophies of India and Persia, traveled in the Eastern expedition of the Roman Emperor, Gordian III, and his ideas reflect their influence. From A.D. 244 he conducted a popular and influential school in Rome, encouraging many to give their wealth to the needy and turn to contemplative thought. Plotinus presented a systematic formulation of Platonic idealistic philosophy in which he conceived of a vast, incomprehensible order that pervaded existence. Unlike the Judeo-Christian concept of creation, in which an eternal God made everything from nothing, Plotinus proposed the concept of emanation, "flowing from": a cosmological concept that explains the creation of the world through a series of emanations or radiations that originate in the godhead. Emanation explains the creation of an imperfect, finite world from an infinite, transcendent god; the world gradually unfolds and emerges through emanations. The flow of divine essence weakens as it flows farther from god. The One, the order that is incomprehensible and self-sufficient, gives rise, through emanations, like ripples emanating from a stone thrown into existence, like a fountain that overflows to lower levels, to the Divine Mind (Logos) that contains all forms, all multiple reflections of the One. Below the Divine Mind is the World Soul, which links the intellectual and material worlds. These three transcendent realities, One, Divine Mind, World Soul, support the finite and visible world. Through ecstatic contemplation in which the soul transcends the restraints of the body, the individual could achieve immediate knowledge of god, or unity with the One.

Neoplatonism influenced early Christianity through St. Augustine, who was a Neoplatonist before his conversion. Its hierarchical model, and the concept of a principle of plenitude that accounts for the complex diversity of the universe, was to have a major impact on the Middle Ages (see, in particular, Lovejoy 1936; Nisbet 1972).

Neoplatonist Dream Theories:
Macrobius's Commentary on Scipio's Dream

The number of books about dreams written between the second and fourth century A.D. reflects a renewed interest in revelatory experience, direct communication with the divine, and the activity of the occult self that Dodds says typifies the "Age of Anxiety." The books also represent a collage of ideas from the classical world concerning the relationship between the soul and the body, especially as expressed by the Neoplatonists. The book from this period that was to have the greatest influence on the Middle Ages, although it was not original, was Macrobius's *Commentarius in Somnium Scipionis*

(Commentary on Scipio's Dream), dating from the end of the fourth century A.D. The work shows obvious historical continuity with the writings that preceded it; dream books in Greece date from at least the fifth century B.C., but most were lost, and their knowledge has come down, secondhand, through the writings of Artemidorus, Macrobius, Synesius, and others.

Ambrosius Theodosius Macrobius was born about A.D. 360 and died after A.D. 422. Besides the *Commentary*, he wrote *On the Differences and Similarities of the Greek and Latin Verb* and a series of dialogues imitating Plato called *Saturnalia,* an incomplete work that sheds light on Roman society at the end of the fourth century.

Scipio's dream, on which Macrobius comments, was the closing episode (ix-xxvi) of Cicero's *De re publica,* which itself was an imitation of Plato's *Republic,* except that instead of writing about an ideal utopia, as Plato did, Cicero was writing specifically about the Roman Republic. As in Plato's work, Cicero organized *De re publica* as a dialogue; this dialogue took place over three days during the Latin holidays in the winter of B.C. 129 in Scipio's home; and Scipio's dream at the end of *De re publica* is a takeoff from the vision of Er at the end of Plato's *Republic*. Macrobius's method is to take an excerpt from Scipio's dream and discuss it at great length. He elaborates on Neoplatonic doctrine, Pythagorean arithmetic, harmony of the spheres, immortality of the soul, and other demonstrations of his encyclopaedic knowledge. In the process, he also develops a five-fold classification of dreams.

Two of these five types of dreams (*visum* and *insomnium*) he said were valueless for moral education. The *visum,* hypnagogic delusion, is a confused and meaningless disturbance of the imaginative faculty which comes when the dreamer is half awake and half asleep. The *insomnium,* a dream produced by mental or physical distress, is worthless because dreams are important only when the dreamer is sleeping.

The only interesting dreams to Microbius are dreams that reveal truth. In an *oraculum,* an imposing authority such as a parent, priest, or god appears and gives the dreamer a clear forecast of the future and advice about what to do. A *visio* is a vision of a future event exactly as it will happen. A *somnium,* an enigmatic dream requiring allegorical interpretation, is a figurative vision of the future. The *somnium* is further divided into five classifications based on possible subject matter: oneself (*somnium proprium*), someone else (*somnium alienum*), oneself and others together (*somnium commune*), a public place or event (*somnium publicum*), and the heavens and the earth (*somnium generale*).

Macrobius's dream categories are not exclusive. Scipio's dream was a *somnium* (containing all five subclassifications), with elements of the *oraculum* and *visio.* The visionary authority appearing in the dream was Scipio Africanus, a great figure from Roman history. In later writings about dreams, such as those by Boethius (of the late fifth and sixth centuries A.D.), these visionary authorities could be allegorical, as in Boethius's Lady Philosophy. The evolution of Macrobius's dream categories, their frequent confusion and reorganization, provides insight into changing conceptions and uses of the dream.

Artemidorus's Interpretation of Dreams

Macrobius's classification of dreams is similar to that of Artemidorus of Daldis, a professional dream interpreter of the second century A.D., whose *Oneirocritica* (*Interpretation of Dreams*) was itself a synopsis of earlier dream books. Artemidorus collected more than three thousand dreams and information on the dreamers' history and character (their occupation and civic function, whether they were citizen or slave, male or female, parent or child), as well as the outcome of their dreams.

The first three books of Artemidorus, intended for the general public, provide a unified and structured treatise on the interpretation of dreams involving knowing extensive details about the dreamer's life and culture. The fourth and fifth books were written for his son, a novice dream interpreter, with instructions not to reproduce them; they constitute a perfunctory study manual. He urged his son to read other interpreters, such as Antiphon of Athens, who specialized in dreams on squids and octopuses; Telmessus of Lycia on teeth; and Alexander of Mynaus on onions, thunderbolts, and swallows (see White 1975); and not to give explanations that were too simple. To impress the public, he recommended the use of elaborate puns and anagrammatical transpositions to interpret dreams, and the use of equal numerical value of names and dream objects.

Artemidorus's first book provides a classification of dreams that in many ways resembles Macrobius's classification two centuries later. It reflects the diverse theories of the second century. He says that often dreams are only a continuation of the day's activities. This idea was common in Epicurean literature, since one of the aims of the school was to undermine the belief of the masses, fostered by the Stoics, that dreams were sent by the gods; it also reflects medical theories, such as those expressed by Hippocrates in *On Dreams* (fourth century B.C.) and by Galen in *On Diagnosis Through Dreams* (second century A.D.), that dreams are the result of indigestion, intoxication, illness, and so on. An *enhypnion* ("something in one's sleep") is limited to sleep and disappears upon waking. These categories correspond to Macrobius's *visum* and *insomnium*. Artemidorus used the word *Oneiros* ("telling what is real") not in the Homeric sense of an objectified dream messenger but as an experience that excites the soul and enables the dreamer to predict future events (Artemidorus 1.1). He accepts the idea that some dreams, especially those with unexpected outcomes, are sent by the gods (*theopempton*). He distinguished between *theorematikoi*, "direct" dreams that come true as they occur in the dream, and *allegorikoi*, dreams that disclose their meanings through symbols--"the soul is conveying something obscurely by physical means" (Artemidorus 1.2). This latter type, what would correspond to Macrobius's *somnium*, has a deeper meaning and may take longer to come true.

The Linkage of Dream, Soul, and the Occult in Neoplatonism

The discussion of the occult soul is a frequent topic of these early dream books. Some stress the classical contrast between body and soul (true dreams are those achieved through the exercise of the divine soul, whereas false dreams are those caused by activities of the body) whereas others reflect the division of the soul into good and evil parts.

The Neoplatonist Iamblichus, reflecting the classical period, distinguished between human and divine dreams (Taylor 1895:115); the divine dream comes when the soul is freed from the body and is thus able to foresee the future and "the most genuine principles of knowledge."

In the second century A.D. a contemporary of Artemidorus, Maximus of Tyre, used the metaphor of the heavenly dream flight to describe the capacity of the soul to transcend the limitations of the body and achieve wisdom--not from wide experience (opinion), but from transcendent, philosophical wisdom (knowledge):

> But to what shall I compare the spectacles of a philosopher? to a clear dream by Jupiter, circularly borne along in all directions; in which . . . the soul travels round the whole earth, from earth ascends to heaven. (*Dissertations* xxviii)

Continuing this metaphor, Maximus describes a man named Aristeas who lay on the ground for three days while his soul wandered in the air surveying the earth. His soul journey, this "beautiful sleep" with "clear dreams," is the act of contemplation by which the soul escapes the body.

Macrobius accepts the Orphic formula that the body is a prison; the soul's descent into the body is a death and a forgetting. He describes the soul as the "true man" (II, xii, 10) and argues for its power of independent knowledge--against the objections of Aristotle (II, xii-xvi). This autonomy makes the revelatory dream possible; in sleep the body's ties are looser and the soul is able to confront truth directly. The soul has an independent noetic power that derives from the dualism of body-soul.

Scipio's dream, like the vision of Er in Plato and the dream of Aristeas in Maximus of Tyre, is dream revelation at its highest--the true dream that confers *gnosis*, an esoteric wisdom beyond the ordinary which initiates man into a way of life that brings him closer to divinity. Dreams provide a form of contemplation which the soul can look forward to when it returns to its "true home." Because of his dream, Scipio gained wisdom beyond that possible through the ordinary operation of the mind.

Macrobius's excerpt from Cicero, the only work of Cicero that was preserved throughout the Middle Ages, was usually appended to Microbius's *Commentary*, even though Cicero also wrote a treatise on dreams, *De Divinatione* (I, 63, 64) clearly reflecting Plato's doctrine that the soul possesses knowledge of the past, present, and future--the visionary power of surveying all time and existence. "When it is called away from the contagion of its bodily associate the soul remembers the past, discerns the present, and foresees the future; for the sleeper's body lies as if dead, while his spirit is alive and in full vigour." Cicero inherited many of the ideas of Posidonius, who had perfected the dream typology of the Stoics. The Stoics specified that dreams had three possible origins: Dreams could originate with the human spirit, with immortal spirits of the air, or with gods. Posidonious also included a fourth category--premonitory dreams--that were divided into two groups, clear or enigmatic. A more complete understanding of Cicero's dream theories occurred during the classicist revival of the Renaissance (for example, a group of Latin literary stylists called the Ciceronians refused to use any word not found in Cicero). But, for the Middle Ages, Cicero was conveyed primarily through Macrobius. His distinction between direct, clear dreams (*visio*) and allegorical, indirect dreams (*somnium*) was useful to early Christians who sought the former and distrusted the latter; but it was his doctrine on the dream allegory that was to have such a major influence in the later Middle Ages. Macrobius influenced Chaucer and the famous dream visions of love in the twelfth century, the thirteenth-century *Romance of the Rose*, and the fourteenth-century *Divine Comedy*. His dream theory "became the key to a renaissance in the study of dreams in the twelfth century, exemplified by the pseudo-Augustine's *De spiritu et anima* and by John of Salisbury's *Policraticus*" (Le Goff 1988:201). He provided a lexicon of visionary poetry that was used by poets, physicians, moralists, and cosmologists for at least one thousand years (see Dahlberg 1971; Fleming 1969, 1984; Stahl 1952). Although highly influential, Macrobius's categories were often confused by later writers; it is more important to look at medieval epistemology and the ways that medieval writers used Macrobius's ideas (see chapter 4).

DIVINE REVELATION AND THE DREAM:
THE CHRISTIAN QUEST FOR VISIO

A confusing melange of classical and Judeo-Christian concepts of true and false dreams is found in the first few centuries of the Christian era. Chalcidius, a fourth-century contemporary of Macrobius, categorizes dreams in a Latin commentary on Plato's *Timaeus* (Chapters 250-256). He distinguishes between dreams sent by God (clear dreams coming directly from God); those that come from God via angels or demons, called *admonito*; those caused by external impression that originate in the soul and have no significance for the future, called *somnium*; and dreams produced by the superior part of the soul but generally obscure, called *visum*. Chalcidius argues that God, whose nature is good, would not refuse to provide humans with guidance through dreams and other forms of communication.

Firmianus Lactantius (ca. A.D. 260-340), sometimes called the "Christian Cicero," converted to Christianity and became the tutor of the eldest son of Constantine about A.D. 306. In his major work, *Divinarum Institutionum Libri Septem*, he suggested that demons were able to get into men's bodies secretly because of their extreme thinness--a Christian adaptation of the Atomist doctrine of Democritus that Cicero wrote about in *De Divinatione* II, viii. All objects give off images--*eidola*--that drift through the air, like dust motes, until they strike an organ of perception such as the human eye. These *eidola* are so thin that they can penetrate the human body and affect the mind, thus stimulating dreams.

The use of dreams to convey one's communication with God, or to portray the progress of one's soul as one wrestled with angels and demons, was an important part of the shamanic, ecstatic process. "Oneiric autobiography" became a literary genre, including works such as Augustine's *Confessions*, Guibert of Norgent's twelfth-century *De vita sua*, and Julio de Baroja's sixteenth-century *Vidas magicas y Inquisicion* (Le Goff 1988:200, 214-216; see Patch 1950 for a description of the iconographic motifs of saints' visions). It is often difficult to tell the degree to which these "dream autobiographies" are personal, or reflect the development of the standardized Everyman allegorical dream vision of the High Middle Ages (see eighth and ninth century dream visions from England and Germany, including the *Vision of Tundane*, *St. Patrick's Purgatory*, and *The Dream of the Rood*). The main difference between the saints' visions and the later allegorical dream visions is that saints represent the hierarchically superior type of person described by Macrobius, able to dream true, revelatory dreams (and, in the Christian context, to be wise enough to detect the difference between dreams sent by God and those sent by demons. But the narrator of the allegorical dream vision is Everyman--a sinner (*Dream of the Rood*), a melancholic fool (Chaucer, *The*

Book of the Duchess), a shallow rake (*Romance of the Rose*), or a lonely, lost, naive, troubled doubter (Dante, *The Divine Comedy*). The purpose of these dream visions is not to demonstrate Christian ecstasy, but to teach Christians the moral order of an established Christianity. The first fully developed allegorical dream visions appear in the second half of the twelfth century, including de Lille's *Anticlaudianus* and *De Planctu Naturae*, followed by *Romance of the Rose* in the thirteenth century, and *The Divine Comedy* in the fourteenth century (see chapter 4).

Ecstatic communion occurs outside the hierarchy of society. Joan of Arc, for example, was burned because she did not recognize the hierarchy of the church but directly communicated with God. In some writings (such as those of Tertullian, the first great Christian theorist of dreams, and Synesius of Cyrene), dreams became the democratic property of all Christians. One did not need to sleep in holy places (incubation), depend on an "oneiromancer," or be an important person. According to Tertullian (160-240 A.D.):

> The force [of the soul or ecstasy] is not circumscribed by the boundaries of sacred places. It wanders, flying here and there, and remains free. No one can doubt that houses are open to demons and that men are encircled by "images" not only in sacred places but even in their rooms (46.13) . . . it is a superstition to prescribe fasting for those who practice incubation near oracles in order to obtain cures. (48.3)

Synesius of Cyrene (ca. 370-414), a Neoplatonist who converted to Christianity and became bishop of Ptolemais, wrote *On Dreams* when he was still a pagan.

Macrobius would probably not have agreed with Tertullian and Synesius. Macrobius conveyed the traditional idea that there is a hierarchy of dreamers; only those with high authority could dream authentic premonitory dreams (although Scipio was not a leader of a city, the distinction of his natural and adoptive fathers, as well as his own distinctive characteristics, qualified him to have an authentic dream). During this period of the decline of the Roman Empire, Macrobius sought to preserve classical knowledge and the social order. Macrobius, in making his commentary on Scipio's dream, argues that the best way to make a person want to lead a law-abiding life is to show him the habitations and rewards of departed souls. As Scipio the Elder says to Scipio who is having the dream, "That you may be more zealous in safeguarding the commonwealth, Scipio, be persuaded of this: all those who have saved, aided, or enlarged the commonwealth have a definite place marked off in the heavens where they may enjoy a blessed existence forever"

Stahl 1952:92). Macrobius's writings reflect the belief current in his day of the eternal destiny of Rome.

Christian Prophetism and the Uses of the Dream

In the prophetic, shamanic, ecstatic quest of early Christianity, dreams and visions are often referred to as direct manifestations of the divine in human life, for example, Joel 2:28-29, "And it shall come to pass afterward, that I will pour out my spirit on all flesh; your sons and your daughters shall prophesy, your old men shall dream dreams, and your young men shall see visions. Even upon the menservants and maidservants in those days, I will pour out my spirit." But in many passages a distinction appears to be made between the vision (*visio*) as a more direct, face-to-face contact with the divine, as compared with the more indirect, allegorical contact (*somnium*). The closer you are to God, the more clearly, and less allegorically, He speaks. Pagans get obscure dream messages, such as the dreams of Pharaoh's butler and baker (Genesis 40:9-19), Pharaoh's dream of the seven sleek cows and the seven gaunt cows (Genesis 41), or Nebuchadnezzar's dreams about the statue of gold, silver, bronze, iron, and clay (Daniel 2:31-35) and the great tree commanded to be cut down by the watcher (Daniel 4:10-17). Moses, however, speaks face-to-face with God in a passage that contrasts both visions and dreams with face-to-face contact:

> And he said, "Hear my words: If there be a prophet among you, I the Lord make myself known to him in a vision, I speak with him in a dream. Not so with my servant Moses; he is entrusted with all my house. With him I speak mouth to mouth, clearly, and not in dark speech; and he beholds the form of the Lord." (Numbers 12:6-8)

Dreams are often portrayed as dangerous illusions, and dream interpreters as false prophets. Moses warns Israel against false prophets and dreamers, emphasizing humanity's personal relationship with God:

> If there arise among you a prophet, or a dreamer of dreams, and giveth thee a sign or a wonder, and the sign or the wonder come to pass, whereof he spake unto thee, saying, Let us go after other gods, which thou hast not known, and let us serve them; thou shalt not hearken unto the words of that prophet, or that dreamer of

dreams: for the Lord your God proveth you, to know whether ye love the Lord your God with all your heart and with all your soul. (Deuteronomy 13: 1-3)

Similar warnings are issued in Jeremiah:

And the Lord said to me, "The prophets are prophesying lies in my name: I did not send them, nor did I command them or speak to them. They are prophesying to you a lying vision, worthless divination, and the deceit of their own minds (14:14). . . . I have heard what the prophets have said who prophesy lies in my name, saying, "I have dreamed, I have dreamed! . . . Let the prophet who has a dream tell the dream, but let him who has my word speak my word faithfully (23:25-28). . . . So do not listen to your prophets, your diviners, your dreamers, your soothsayers, or your sorcerers, who are saying to you, 'You shall not serve the king of Babylon." (27:9). . . . "Do not let your prophets and your diviners who are among you deceive you, and do not listen to the dreams which they dream, for it is a lie which they are prophesying to you in my name; I did not send them," says the Lord. (29:8-9).

In the apocalyptic writings of Zechariah (10:2), the people wander like sheep because "the diviners see lies; the dreamers tell false dreams, and give empty consolation."

During the period when Christianity was struggling to be established, rival sects emphasized visions and dreams as a means to contact God directly and foresee the future. The Ebionites or Nazarenes were a Judeo-Christian sect, descendants of the first Christian community in Jerusalem, who crossed the Jordan to Pella between A.D. 66-70 and were early believers in gnostic beliefs. Other rivals to Christianity were the Valentinian and Capocrates gnostics of the mid-second century, and the followers of Montanus, a Phrygian who between A.D. 160 and 170 gave prophetic warnings during ecstatic trances.

Tertullian (A.D. 160-240), the first great Christian theorist of dreams, joined the Montanists around A.D. 205. Ecstasy played an important role in his dream typology. Between A.D. 210 and 213 when he was a Montanist, Tertullian composed a treatise on dreams, preserved in chapters 47-49 of *De anima*. He distinguishes between *visio* and *somnium*. For example, in *De anima* 47.2 he says, "Most men owe their knowledge of God to visions," whereas *somnia* are the business of sleep. Dreams derive from the activity of the soul (see chapter 4), but true and false dreams are not to be distinguished by the body-soul dualism but by their origin from God or the Devil. Dreams from the Devil are vain, deceitful, and licentious, whereas those from God are true, prophetic, and enlightening. Although it is the natural property of the soul to be active (and dreams are proof of the activity of the soul), only saints are capable of distinguishing between dreams from God and dreams from the Devil.

The martyrs Perpetua and Saturus were associated with Tertullian; some have suggested that he was the author of *Passio S. Perpetuae et Felicitatis,* a description of five visions experienced in prison (four by Perpetua and one by Saturus).

St. Perpetua, a woman who converted to Christianity and was martyred at Carthage in A.D. 202-203, had four dreams while she was waiting to be executed. In the first dream, she sees a ladder bristling with arms rising up to heaven, with a dragon at its foot; Saturus helps her to mount this dragon, which carries her to a large garden where she is welcomed by a shepherd dressed in white who gives her cheese to eat (Le Goff 1988:205). This vision is shown to her as a result of her deciding that she is worthy to converse with God. Her brother says, "Honored sister, you already possess such great merit that you are worthy of asking for a vision, and you will be shown whether it is martyrdom or release that awaits us," and she interprets the dream to mean martyrdom is her fate. In the second and third dreams her long-dead baby brother occupies an unfriendly garden in the other world, a glimpse of what later becomes Purgatory, according to Le Goff (1984:205). In the fourth dream, she defeats the Devil who appears in the form of an Egyptian, and she is rewarded not with Christian symbolism but with the golden apples of the Hesperides. The dream of Satyrus is more stereotyped and contains conventional Christian imagery, such as angels carrying off the soul.

Tertullian, in developing a Christian doctrine on dreams, said that most dreams are sent by demons (chapter 47). Occasionally good demons send true and profitable dreams, but most of them are "vain, deceptive, disturbing, and ludicrous." God also sends prophetic dreams that are available, as Synesius suggests, to most humans, even to children and pagans such as the Atlantes of Libya; but the dreamer should beware the dreams sent by evil demons, who even try to tempt the saints. Another type of dream is that instigated by the soul itself in response to circumstances (the sleeper's body, his diet, his degree of sobriety, etc.). Like other Christians of his time, including the heretical Montanists, he adds a fourth type of dream, the type associated with ecstasy.

St. Cyprian, an orthodox bishop of the third century, said that God is present in every Christian via dreams, visions, and that supreme form of dream known to few Christians, ecstasy:

That is why the divine governance is constantly correcting us night and day. In addition to nocturnal visions, by day the Holy Spirit fills us in ecstasy with the innocence of children and makes us see with our eyes, hear, and speak the admonitions and instruction that God makes us worthy to receive. (Cyprian, Epistle 9, PL 4.253)

Important people such as bishops (himself included) are favored by God to receive visions.

During the two centuries that preceded the recognition of Christianity as an official religion in the fourth century, dreams played a role in conversion (see Dodds 1965:38-46). Origen (A.D. 185-254) wrote about visions or dreams being responsible for conversion (*Contra Celsum* 1.46): "Many came to Christianity in spite of themselves, a certain spirit having turned their hearts from hatred of the doctrine to resolution to die for it by presenting them with a vision or dream." Christian apocalyptic literature of the first few centuries of the Christian era describe many out-of-body experiences, journeys to the other world, that are sometimes considered "miracles," and sometimes revelations through dream visions. This journey later becomes conceptualized as a journey, by means of a dream, between death and the afterlife, between damnation and salvation (Dante's *Divine Comedy*).

The Bible itself recognizes the divine aspects of dreams and visions. Dreams were one of the few forms of divination that continued to be accepted by Christianity, although one had to be careful to distinguish between true and false dreams, and between true and false prophets. In Acts 16:9-10:

a vision appeared to Paul in the night: a man of Macedonia was standing beseeching him and saying, "Come over to Macedonia and help us." And when we had seen the vision, immediately we sought to go on into Macedonia, concluding that God had called us to preach the gospel to them."

Direct visitations play an important role in early Christian accounts of dreams. For example, Natalius the Confessor was saved from heresy by a dream in which holy angels whipped him all night, and Gregory of Nyssa was scolded by the Forty Martyrs in a dream and turned to a life of contemplation as a result. Dreams were also important in the history of the establishment of Christianity. In acceptable Church history they are considered deciding factors in Constantine's battle at Milvian Bridge, and in Theodosius's battle with Eugenius. In the battle fought by Theodosius, a soldier is said to have had the same vision, which Theodosius uses to bolster his claim that the dream is true rather than false.

The Dream and the Catholic Church

After Christianity became the official religion, ecstatic, personal visions became less acceptable, as illustrated by what happened to Joan of Arc; and dreams "were viewed with suspicion because they were seen as a way of circumventing the Church's role as mediator" (Le Goff 1988:213).   Only kings or saints (such as Constantine, Theodosius, Charlemagne, and St. Perpetua) could have personal, ecstatic, direct confrontation with God, demons, or angels in dreams. In the monasteries, records were kept of the dreams of monks such as John Cassian of Marseilles (fifth century A.D.) and Bede the Venerable in Britain (seventh and eighth centuries), but these were largely private until the urban revolution and changes in monastic orders. In the accounts of these dreams, the terms vary, the categories of Macrobius becoming more confused. But whether *visio, somnium, sopor* (light sleep), the Hebrew *tardema* (deep sleep), or *somnus cum ecstasi* (sleep with ecstasy) were used, the more indirect, allegorical visions of Macrobius's *somnium* were less trusted than the direct visitations of a holy person from Christian iconography.

Between the fifth and seventh centuries, Christian dream categories were rigidified by the writings of Gregory the Great (A.D. 540-604) and Isidore of Seville (A.D. 570-636). In his *Dialogues* (4.50) written in 593-594, Gregory says that "oneiric images" may derive from a full or empty stomach (*ventris plenitudine* or *inanitate*), from delusions *(illusione)*, or from revelation *(revelatione)*. They may come from several sources at the same time ("mixed dreams"), such as a combination of thought and delusion (*cogitatione simul et illusione*) or thought and revelation (*cogitatione simul et revelatione*), which makes it almost impossible for ordinary dreamers to interpret them. Also, delusions are caused by the "hidden enemy"--the Devil. Only saints are capable of deciding whether dreams come from "good spirits" sent by God, or "illusions" sent by the Devil. They are favored with true dreams, divine revelations, and clear visions rather than ones that are obscure *(occulte)*. Numerous *exempla*, brief moralistic anecdotes that became common during the Middle Ages, warned against giving importance to dreams, for one might be deceived by the Devil (Le Goff 1988:224).

In the *Sententiae* (3:6), Isidore of Seville portrays prayer as being a remedy for dreams in which one is tempted by the Devil. Demons use dreams to weaken men; they send tempting illusions that only saints can resist.

Dreams, however, had another significance that came to be extremely important during the High Middle Ages. For this understanding of dream, we must understand medieval epistemology as it developed from St. Augustine's Neoplatonic-adapted concept of levels of vision (see chapter 4).

4

Medieval Epistemology and Allegory

This, then, is how I won my vermeil Rose.
Then morning came, and from my dream at last I woke.
Guillame de Lorris and Jean de Meun,
The Romance of the Rose

THE CRYSTALLIZATION OF WESTERN CULTURE
DURING THE MIDDLE AGES

The term "Middle Ages," as discussed in the first chapter, implies a middle position between the "Ancient World" and the "Modern World." During the first four centuries of the Christian era, as we saw in the previous chapter, a number of syntheses of classical and Christian concepts occurred. Between 476 (when Roman imperial authority ended) and the late seventh and early eighth centuries (when the Carolingians emerged in Frankland), Western civilization was being built on Greco-Roman, Christian, and the Germanic heritage of the barbarian successor states that took over the political authority of Rome. During the ninth and tenth centuries Europe was faced with onslaughts from the Vikings in the north, Hungarians from the east, and Saracens from the south, which stimulated unification.

By about 1050 invasions had stopped and Europe had evolved into a coherent unity dominated by the Catholic Church. During the High Middle Ages (1050-1300) the papacy was weakened by its involvement with secular politics (a process reflected in Dante's *Divine Comedy*), and new monastic movements developed. Commerce threatened feudalism and promoted the rise of towns; new cathedrals were built, as were universities (linked with "universe"--see Curtius 1953:54-55).

During the Middle Ages, Western culture emerged from a dialectic involving continued attempts to integrate classical and Christian thought and to reconcile reason and faith. The creation of medieval conceptions of the world, the attempt to create a wholeness to an emerging cultural unit (reminiscent of Germany's quest for *kultur* as a unifying psychological spirit of a people, reflecting a nationalistic trend when Germany was a dispersed set of petty kingdoms), was reflected in encyclopaedic expressions-- *Mappaemundi*, elaborate renditions of the lives of saints or classical philosophers, and encyclopaedic dream visions. The Neoplatonists did the same thing when classical and Christian thought were rivals. During the Renaissance, early printed books consisted in massive collections of aphorisms, the oral learning of a nonliterate age (see Speroni 1968). Nineteenth-century writers, coming to terms with Romantic and Enlightenment principles, produced elaborate tomes. One of the most encyclopaedic efforts being made today is in the field of anthropology, which is categorized as belonging to both the sciences and the humanities. Sometimes referred to as "the last refuge of Renaissance man," anthropology could equally be referred to as the last refuge of Neoplatonic man. Today's anthropologists are attempting to integrate all human activity into a complex whole and are covering the evolutionary history of humankind as well as its cross-cultural diversity.

MEDIEVAL EPISTEMOLOGY

The confusion that occurred with Macrobius's categories of dreaming had to do with medieval epistemology, or medieval theories of knowledge. What exactly was a *visio*? What was the meaning of "clear vision"? How did humans see and know reality?

Dreams provided a complex metaphor for expressing medieval concepts of "seeing" and knowing. According to Macrobius, dreams are caused by many factors, but important dreams are those that result from the activity of the soul. Tertullian, although he accepted Macrobius's distinction between *visio* and *somnium*, stated the Christian doctrine on dreams:

> they are born from the accidents of sleep and the significant movements of the soul, which as we have said is always busy and agitated because of its perpetual movement, due to its divine and immortal character. Hence when rest comes to the body as its peculiar comfort, the soul, for which this comfort is not intended,

does not rest and, since it must do without the activity of the body's members, uses its own. (*De anima* 45, quoted in Le Goff 1988:275)

The early Christian poet Aurelius Clemens Prudentius, inspired by Tertullian, expressed similar ideas in his poetry. In *Hamartigenia*, a poem about the origin of sin, dreams are proof that the soul is immortal. Because of the soul's divine nature, dreams offer insight into truth. The soul has the power of vision; it is freed from the dark veil in which the body enshrouds it.

According to St. Augustine, there are three types of vision of which the soul is capable. This thesis was developed in *De Genesi ad Litteram*, which discussed "visions and revelations of the Lord" described by St. Paul:

I know a man in Christ who fourteen years ago was caught up to the third heaven--whether in the body or out of the body I do not know, God knows. And I know that this man was caught up into Paradise--whether in the body or out of the body I do not know, God knows--and he heard things that cannot be told, which man may not utter. (II Cor. 12:2-5)

In discussing the mystery of whether the man came to see and know paradise in or out of the body, Augustine distinguishes between three types of vision: *corporale* (the ordinary vision of the eye and of the body's senses), *spiritale* (the imaginative vision of the soul by which the soul can "see" corporeal things that are not physically present), and *intellectuale* (the vision of the intellect by which the soul can "see" things that have no bodily image, as in Platonic Ideas and mathematical relationships). These types of seeing exist in a hierarchical relationship to one another, and are a part of humankind's constant striving toward understanding of the divine: Everything one sees with the eyes or experiences with the senses imprint themselves on the soul, creating a spiritual image that is then milked for its non-body meaning by the intellect. The concept is an obvious application of Plotinus's Neoplatonic concept of emanations and his unified, hierarchical concept of the One from which issues the diverse world, except that Augustine is working backwards, from the corporeal World Soul to the One.

With this classification of different types of vision, Augustine could interpret various visions in the Bible. Moses experienced a corporeal vision when he saw the burning bush, whereas the man who was taken up into the third heaven had experienced an intellectual vision ("he heard things that cannot be told, which man may not utter"). Most visions in the Bible belong to the second category of vision, the spiritual vision (corporeal images that lack body, that are images). In this framework of knowing, the difference between true and false dreams lies not in the difference between clear and unclear (*visio* and allegorical *somnium*). Some ideas are, by their very nature, unclear, because they belong to a higher form of knowing. The dream, as an activity of the soul, begins the process by which the dreamer ascends the hierarchical ladder of knowing (confronting, in the process, demons that try to mislead the activity of his soul).

Augustine's ideas are reflected in the writings of Synesius (ca. 370-414), who suggests that the corporeal world is a visible manifestation of *Nous*, the mind of God (Crawford 1901; Fitz-Gerald 1930). The soul has the power to move from observation of the corporeal to understanding of divine reason by virtue of its ability to see images (imagination). The ability to see images lies at the border "between reason and unreason, between the bodiless and the body" (Fitz-Gerald 1930:334).

The dream, as the activity of the soul, became a bridge to ways of knowing, and in the form of the dream vision of the High Middle Ages became a potent symbolic vehicle for expressing medieval ways of knowing. The dream, like sleeping and waking, became powerful metaphors, used in the form of allegories (representations of abstract or spiritual meaning through material form), in medieval culture. The allegory, because it deals with images of the corporeal, provides a bridge between what is known by the senses and the noncorporeal enlightenment of divine intellect. Allegory is the veiling of truth in images (see Osgood 1956). Allegory is a vitally important form of expressing ideas because that is how humans think--from the concrete to the abstract, as we would say today, or in Neoplatonic-medieval terms, from the corporeal to the intellectual. In this context the dream vision is itself an allegory of the Augustinian-medieval concept of allegory.

According to Prudentius, Christ was a cock whose crow woke humans from the sleep of sin. Sometimes dreams were portrayed as illusions of corporeal life, but often they were portrayed as the activity of the soul in search of divine understanding. The "sleeping" man (the pagan, the unconverted drugged with ignorance, the sinner doomed to die before he reaches knowledge of God, or Everyman, confused and mired in the cares of the world) "awakes" to a dream. Through the dream vision he ascends from corporeal to spiritual to intellectual levels of knowing, and at the end of the vision "awakes" to a higher level of understanding.

The passage from heresy to orthodoxy, sin to salvation, evil to good, was symbolized as a transition from sleeping to waking. St. Augustine made famous Paul's exhortation in Romans:

We know the time, that it is the hour for us to awake from sleep. Our salvation is now nearer than we had believed. The night is far spent, and the day approaches. Let us therefore put off the works of darkness and put on the armour of light . . . put on the Lord Jesus Christ, and make no provision for the flesh, to fulfill its lusts. (Chapter 13: 11-12)

Medieval writings made extensive use of this analogy. During the "sleep" of humankind's phenomenal existence or unawakened state of existence, humans could receive visions or dreams that represented the signs of salvation, the path of righteousness, or the wages of sin. The medieval dream vision was a standard mode of organizing allegorical representations of the Christian view of reality. The dream vision symbolized a state of transcendence, a borderline between "noumena and phenomena" in which one might achieve an understanding of eternal truths, portrayed allegorically, or catch a brief, blinding light of the divine communicating directly through the dream. Humans were mired in the decaying, illusory, corporeal world of the senses, but through visionary, spiritual dreams could catch a glimpse of the divine other that was working out a plan by which good sought to conquer evil.

Alain de Lille (ca. 1128-1202), a French theologian and Latinist who earned the title *Doctor universalis* for his extensive learning, applied St. Augustine's classification of ways of seeing to an understanding of dreams. Dreams could be idle (corporeal), imaginative (spiritual), or contemplative (intellectual). His poetic treatise on arts and morals, *Anticlaudianus*, describes a dream allegory reminiscent of Dante's *Divine Comedy* (see Raby 1953, Wright 1872). In search of a soul, the female protagonist, Prudence, makes a journey to God. Dream journeys are usually made upward in medieval dream visions--toward the heavens, up a mountain--although as we will see in *Romance of the Rose*, journeys may begin in a garden. She is guided first by Reason as far as the heavenly stars, then by Theology to God's court, and then by Faith into God's presence. In God's presence she swoons but is revived by Faith with medicine made from poppies, a substance that would normally create lethargy, but here is linked with transcendence of the body and the knowledge gained in the ultimate stages of contemplation (she "awakens" through sleep).

De Lille's *De planctu naturae*, a satire on human vices, begins as Nature wakens the sleeping narrator, who thereby enters the dream vision, and ends with an additional awakening--into greater understanding as a result of the vision.

Rhetoric, Memory, and Allegory

The use of rhetoric and allegorical methods of organizing memory was a standard method of organizing information before the development of printing. The Middle Ages inherited techniques from the Greeks and Romans, and the emphasis on memory continued until the development of printing caused it to decline (see Boorstin 1984)--although it took quite awhile (see Speroni 1968 and chapter 5). Plato emphasized the ability of the soul to remember ideal forms. For example, in the Meno, Plato expounded the doctrine of *anamnesis* whereby he argued that mathematical ideas exist in the uneducated mind, like Jung holding dreams up to the light in search of racial-memory archetypes. According to Cicero, memory was one of the five principle parts of rhetoric. Rhetoric was the mode by which history, philosophy, and science were learned, especially in the curriculum proposed by Martianus Capella in the fifth century in his work, *Satyricon* or *De Nuptiis Philologioe et Mercurii et de septem Artibus liberalibus libri novem*. As an encyclopaedia of the culture of his time, it included ideas that were to influence medieval thinkers for ten centuries. For example, a passage in Book viii contains a reference to the heliocentric system of astronomy and may have influenced Copernicus. The work is an allegory about the marriage of Mercury to a nymph, Philologia. The seven liberal arts that constitute human knowledge--the Trivium: Grammar, Rhetoric, and Dialectic, and the Quadrivium: Arithmetic, Geometry, Astronomy, and Music--are their courtiers.

The art of memory influenced the way cathedrals were built. During the Renaissance, the revival of the Neoplatonists resulted in a similar emphasis on memory-science (see chapter 5). For example, Giordano Bruno (1548-1600) in *On the Shadows of Ideas* (1582) suggested that zodiac images were closer to enduring reality than the actual arrangement of stars and proposed a system of remembering these ideas that would put humans in closer touch with a higher reality.

The development of allegory in the Middle Ages must be understood in the context of this orientation toward memory. Allegory builds up the kernel of an idea to full, expanded dimensions. Digressions are part of the development of a complete image, rather than a detraction from the narrative, as they are during the age of printing. As in music, one plays variations on a theme so that the theme will be remembered. The Church fathers explored the concealed spiritual meanings conveyed in biblical narrative, and the allegorical mode was extended from biblical exegesis to the arts in general.

In the psychology of the Middle Ages, reason was an essential aspect of human understanding, and allegory enabled man to move up the hierarchy from the body to divine reason. The numerous allegories in which dream visions play a central role were a mode of conveying and reinforcing the hier-archical, authoritative dictates of a society dominated by the Christian church. The allegories in which acceptable dreams conveyed their divine message were the major mode by which the battle between good and evil forces for the historically rooted human soul was conveyed. This is different from the personal, ecstatic process by which an individual converts, pro-gressing from sin to salvation by wrestling with demons in dreams. The allegory of the dream vision is not for saints but for Everyman, an encyclopaedic, condensed allegory of man's fate. The *somnium*, already accepted as a figurative message to be deciphered, was used in the most powerful allegorical literature of the Middle Ages: the *Romance of the Rose* by Guillame de Lorris and Jean de Meun in the thirteenth century, and Dante's *Divine Comedy* of the fourteenth century.

De Meun, one of the authors of *Romance of the Rose*, translated Boethius's *Consolation of Philosophy* before he wrote *Rose*. Through a dialogue between a doctor and a sick man, Lady Philosophy leads Boethius to understand the vanity and mutability of all things and their resultant false happiness; true happiness lies outside worldly prosperity. De Meun, in his commentary, linked passionate love with the folly of Fortune (a popular theme in late medieval and Renaissance literature).

Macrobius's categories of the dream and Augustine's classifications of types of vision were used to bridge the gap between actual, revelatory, historical appearance of divine personages (mystical revelations), and the rationalistic symbolism of allegories. The vehicle of the allegory could be used by mystics seeking the divine in human history; or, during the Renaissance, as a bridge in the process of secularization by which the grammarians and the rhetoricians constructed humanistic, man-centered (not god-centered) interpretations of the complexity of existence. Under the cloak of allegory, ecclesiastical and worldly subjects could be treated together; it was a way of transcending the church's emphasis on other-worldliness (Vossler 1966:134). It salvaged, preserved, and transmitted the fragments of classical antiquity and the medieval dialogues. It enabled medieval writers to write world histories. For example, allegorical parallelism was first used by Paulus Orosius in 418 who pointed out a mystical connection between Babylonian rule, the Roman Empire, and Chris-tianity. Dante used Orosius and repeats his statement that Christ was born in the same year that Caesar Augustus brought universal peace on earth.

The allegorical dream vision also enabled medieval thinkers to integrate reason and blind faith (*pistis*), the rationality of the world order with ecstasy. The world order was unified by love, the mystical union that surpasseth understanding; and in ascending the hierarchical levels of knowing, one at-tained the Rose, the allegorical representation of this union.

Reason, Faith, and the Beginnings
of Doubt: Scholasticism

For a fuller understanding of the significance of the popularity and controversy surrounding the thirteenth-century allegorical dream vision called *The Romance of the Rose*, and as an introduction to concepts important in understanding the changes that occurred in the semantics, syntactics, and pragmatics of the dream during the Renaissance, a discussion of medieval epistemology should include a review of Scholasticism and a brief forecast of Rationalism during the Renaissance.

Scholasticism formally begins with St. Anselm of the eleventh century A.D., but is rooted in St. Augustine, who integrated Plato with Christianity, and Boethius, who translated and commented on Aristotle in the fifth and sixth centuries A.D.). St. Anselm's motto was "Faith seeking understanding," that is, use reason to illuminate faith. *The Book of Sentences* compiled by Peter Lombard during the early twelfth century became the classical source for medieval thinkers of the church fathers, especially St. Augustine.

Scholasticism classifies the great discourse on rationalism that occurred during the Middle Ages in an effort to prove that faith and reason were compatible. One of St. Anselm's arguments was that God must exist because the highest being our minds can conceive of must exist. The Scholastics were concerned, like Plato, with the Idea as a pattern that precedes the Thing (the forerunner of Rationalism). Obviously deriving from Augustine, Scholasticism conceived of God as thinking Himself, as seeing all possible participations and imitations. Divine ideas are all things creatable and knowable; everything is possible in creative eternity.

In the universities, the two traditional forms of scholastic literature were developed: the question, in which a thesis is proposed and defended against objections, and the commentary. The *summa* was an important medieval literary genre that presented theology and philosophy with great scope and learning. The first *summa* was *On Sacraments* by Hugh of St. Victor, a German scholar and mystic who urged the study of every branch of learning, and who was sometimes called the "second Augustine."

The emphasis on reason was a symptom of the changes going on in the structure of the Church, and ultimately had dangerous consequences for Church authority. One of the most widely debated question during twelfth-century philosophy concerned what was universal. Was there a reality that existed independent of the minds of God and man (the extreme realism of William of Champeaux)? Or did universals exist only in the mind of God, as patterns by which He creates particular things? When Peter Abelard, in the twelfth century, expressed the relativistic view that the universal was a symbol to which humans have attached a commonly agreed significance based on similarities that they perceive in different objects, he was condemned (see McCallum 1976).

The thirteenth century was the golden age of medieval philosophy. Aristotle was extremely influential during the thirteenth century, having been introduced to the West through the translations and commentaries of Arabs such as Avicenna and Averroes. Like the Scholastics, he was systematic and organized in his thinking and research. For instance, in *On Dreams* and *On Divination in Sleep*, he was coolly rational toward dreams, considering them a by-product of natural rather than supernatural processes. The University of Paris became a leading center for the study of Aristotle. Although papal authority forbade the teaching of some of his works in 1210 and 1215, bans against him were lifted in 1240. One of the first important Aristotelians was Albertus Magnus, a student of natural sciences as well.

Although the first author of *The Romance of the Rose* was a devotee of courtly love, the second author was a product of the Scholasticism of the University of Paris. In the next chapter, the relationship between these two methods (statement of the question and development of a commentary) and ideas (what is the nature of God, and how is He reflected in the world?) will be discussed.

New religious orders, the Mendicant Orders of the Dominicans and Franciscans, helped to expand the universities and spread Scholasticism. In contrast with the ancient Benedictines and the more recent Cistercians who lived a contemplative life in the seclusion of monasteries, the Mendicant Orders were dedicated to an active life. They took a vow of poverty and served as wandering preachers. One of their most famous members was Thomas Aquinas, a Dominican.

St. Thomas Aquinas (1225-1274) produced a vast amount of precise, detailed, and organized philosophical work. A kind of Christianized Aristotle, he rejected his secular interpretations but embraced the idea that reason could lead humans to great spiritual truths. He denied that there was any basic conflict between faith and reason. In *Summa Theologica*, Aquinas asks what the consequences of evil were for the existence of God. If natural things can be explained by nature, and voluntary things by the human will, there is no need to suppose God's existence. Aquinas appears to have issued a challenge that Descartes takes up, with fierce doubt engendered by the consequences of Scholastic methods of thinking, during the seventeenth century. But Aquinas provides proof that God exists, beginning with the fact that the world is in motion and therefore requires a first mover, a first cause. He quotes Augustine: God is infinitely good, so He allows evil to exist.

Aquinas established important principles by which Reason could be allied to Theology. Although the reputation of medieval philosophy declined after the fifteenth century, a revival of Thomistic thinking occurred in the late fifteenth century, and every Catholic university included his ideas as part of its curriculum until secularization of the universities in the eighteenth century. A papal encyclical of 1879 urged the study of Aquinas during a revival of Neoscholastics.

William of Occam, the last of the great medieval thinkers, separated religion and philosophy and said there was no rational grounds for faith. According to Jacques Maritain (1969:90), a Neoscholastic French Catholic philosopher, Aristotle established the essential principles of metaphysics according to the demands of reason, Aquinas joined that metaphysics with theology, and in the seventeenth century Descartes, seeking a truth independent of pagan antiquity, removed metaphysics from philosophy and theology from its dominant position. Maritain suggests that we are now watching the "failure of three centuries of rationalism" and argues for a return to the integration of faith with reason. As we will see in chapter 6, Descartes continues many of the traditions of medieval Scholasticism, but he represents the movement during the Renaissance that ultimately promoted secularization of the divine.

The major allegorical dream visions that were being written against the background of the medieval epistemology just discussed in this chapter shall now be described and discussed.

5

The Romance of the Rose
and Other Allegorical
Dream Visions:
Medieval and Modern Voices

Although Dante's *Divine Comedy* is usually thought of as the epitome of the allegorical dream vision of the Middle Ages, it was preceded by *The Romance of the Rose*, the most widely read and influential vernacular poems of the Middle Ages. The intellectual context in which it was published and the controversy that surrounded it over the centuries provide an effective forum for discussing Western culture, as seen through the dream, in the High Middle Ages and after.

THE ALLEGORY OF THE ROSE:
LOVE AND SEX IN THE MEDIEVAL DREAM VISION

The Romance of the Rose (*Roman de la Rose*)

The Romance of the Rose was written by two authors, Guillame de Lorris, who wrote over four thousand verses before the mid-thirteenth century, and Jean de Meun, who added eighteen thousand verses toward the end of the thirteenth century, after Lorris's death. It is the first major French narrative poem that uses first-person narration throughout (it is written from the point of view of the Foolish Lover), and is filled with references to earlier classical and medieval writers.

The term *romance* comes from Old French *parler romanz*, to speak Romance, that is, the vulgar Latin dialect of everyday life as distinguished from book Latin. According to Hollister (1973: 274), medieval vernacular literature resulted from the fusion of two French traditions: the *chanson de geste* of northern France and lyric poetry of southern France. Earlier

Germanic poems of bloodshed and brotherhood-in arms influenced the northern French tradition, exemplified by the eleventh-century *Song of Roland* which integrates the heroic, honor-ridden spirit of early Germany with the Christian dimension. Lyric poetry of southern France, probably of Islamic inspiration, is marked by wit and an emphasis on romantic love. Guillame de Lorris represented this courtly tradition. His verses, about a Lover's erotic passion for his Rose, followed the conventions of the long-suffering lover established by the end of the twelfth century. He sees his Rose and spends the rest of the poem pursuing her.

Jean de Meun was a devotee of Scholastic love rather than of courtly love (Dunn 1962:xvii). He was a product of the University of Paris, a student of the seven liberal arts, and a universal scholar. Each part of the poem represents a different narrative style: a tapestried romance and a Swiftian satire (Luria 1982).

The Scholastic method, as we saw in the previous chapter, provides endless disputations, matches thesis with antithesis, proposes a question and then responds with an elaborate commentary, and engages in the *quodlibet*--questioning on "whatever you wish." *Rose* is a clear representation of this mode. After the Lover sees the Rose, he is shot by the God of Love with five arrows, each of which has allegorical significance, and swears fealty to this god. The Rose's responsiveness, "Fair Welcome," encourages him; her sense of modesty, "Shame," fends him off. Each allegorical personification in the poem defends its role, interprets, quotes authorities, disputes, refutes, defines, and rationalizes. Reason reveals love's folly, Genius argues its necessity, Forced Abstinence says renunciation is unhealthy, and so on, until every aspect of love has been presented.

Writers argue whether or not *The Romance of the Rose* may be treated as an example of Macrobius's concept of an insignificant *insomnium* or *visum*, or as a dream-allegory (*somnium*). *Rose*, as part of its encyclopaedic coverage of the knowledge of this time, reviews the diversity of Macrobius's categories (see Dunn 1962:3).

The Lover, near Narcissus's fountain, sees a rosebush with a beautiful rose, almost as if it is the image of the rose in the fountain, illogical and dreamlike (the image of an image). The Rose is explicitly referred to as an allegorical representation of the lady that the Lover wishes to win (see Dunn 1962:44-45).

The full-blown rose is a recurring iconographic device symbolizing love, a preeminent symbol of generosity and beauty, a living demonstration of divine plenitude, and a symbol of mystical union with the divine. It is an important symbol (see Seward 1960) in Dante's *Divine Comedy*, in Calderon de la Barca's Renaissance drama, *Life's a Dream*, in the turn-of-the-century writings of Yeats (1965) and Rilke (see Bullock-Kimball 1987), and in numerous twentieth-century writings, including Charles L. Harness's science-fiction classic, *The Rose*, and Jean Genet's *Miracle of the Rose*.

Authors differ in their interpretation of the tone of *Rose* and in their interpretation of whether the God of Love to whom the Lover swears fealty is the pagan god, Cupid, or a manifestation of all the reflections of love from carnal to divine (see Dunn 1962:3-4).

Does *Rose* represent a fabulous narrative that, according to Macrobius's classification, describes the unworthy actions of deities or monstrosities that should be disregarded by philosophers? Or does it represent the second, more noble and acceptable type of fabulous narrative, "a decent and dignified conception of holy truths, with respectable events and characters . . . presented beneath a modest veil of allegory"? (Stahl 1952:85). Perhaps Umberto Eco's *The Name of the Rose* parodies this question, following to an absurd end the constant unpeeling of layers in the human search for meaning.

Love, Sex, and the Fate of the Rose

Rose was enormously popular during the fourteenth century, but by the end of the century it faced increasing hostility, which Maxwell Luria (1982) attributes to a developing French humanism and to rivalry among intellectual and religious groups of the time. Around 1400, Christine de Pisan and Jean Gerson attacked *Rose*, linking it with Ovid's poetry as a handbook for men to deceive and seduce women (Dunn 1952:39). Jean Gerson (1362-1428), an anti-Scholastic theologian and chancellor of the University of Paris, wrote a treatise against *Rose* in the form of a dream vision. Christine de Pisan wrote *Le Dit de la Rose* to promote the founding of an *Ordre de la Rose* to honor courtesy and love and to defend women; the society called *Cour Amoureuse* had over six hundred members, many eminent in society, who pledged to honor ladies and cultivate poetry.

Gerson and de Pisan criticized *Rose* for its erotic passages and for what they perceived to be its insulting attitude toward women. The final passages of *Rose*, with its invasion of ivory towers, quivering limbs, spilled seed, and engorged bud, easily qualify for an entry of historical significance in *Playboy* (see Ellis 1900, who condensed the final assault on the Rose into an anemic, bowdlerized conclusion, moving the original verses into an appendix, declaring that anyone who understood French would know why he refused to translate them).

The critics were even more dismayed by passages that demeaned women by saying that heroic women such as Penelope, who resisted the assaults of suitors while Odysseus wandered the world, and Lucretia, a Roman woman who killed herself after being raped, no longer existed.

The poem suggests that if women were chaste, God would have to create mankind anew. Thus the Lover, pursuing his divine mission, assaults the tower with the staff given him by Nature and gains the Rose, after which he thanks the God of Love, Venus, and Fair Welcome--but not Reason.

In 1483, Jean Molinet wrote a prose version of *Rose* in which he gave the highly idiosyncratic interpretation that conquering the Rose at the end of the poem was the cutting of Christ's body from the Cross. Each section is followed by a moral, summarized in a table, to represent Christian history and doctrine. Three editions were issued between 1500 and 1521.

The Renaissance, as will be seen in the following chapter, demonstrated many contradictory tendencies. On the one hand it continued the medieval emphasis on love, continuing to perceive the physical beloved as a shadow of the divine (but with trends toward worldly delight). Twenty-one printed editions of *Rose* were published between 1481 and 1538, and it was familiar to Rabelais and Ronsard of the sixteenth century. Some of these editions, like that of Molinet, restricted the meaning of *Rose* to biblical themes, or attacked it as obscene, whereas others, such as the 1495-1496 edition of the Italian scholar and diplomat Mario Equicola, treated *Rose* as a systematic instruction on the complexities of love. Luria (1982:73) suggests that Rabelais's work in the sixteenth century was what *Rose* was in the thirteenth, the Bible of freethinkers, a political, religious, and philosophical satire in the French tradition. As more effective forms of satire developed, *Rose* was considered old-fashioned.

The Reformation brought increased asceticism and charges of "obscenity," and many editions of *Rose* were mutilated. An illustration of Nature perpetuating the species in a 1370 edition was cut by what Fleming (1969:135) presumes to have been a pious post-Reformation monastic librarian: The only part of the picture that is left is the upper right-hand corner where God appears in an attitude of benediction. "What was good enough for God in 1370 had become shocking to His servants two centuries later" (Fleming 1969:136).

During the late Middle Ages and the Renaissance, *Rose* appears to have been used in a variety of ways, typical of a dominant symbol (see Parman 1990). The mania for allegory that dominated the Middle Ages constituted the science of this time, and *Rose* was mined for multiple meanings. It had moral or religious significance, even astrological and alchemical significance. During the Renaissance, the science of allegory evolved into a science of mythology. The French Pleiad (see chapter 6) incorporated *Rose* in the French mythological tradition of the sixteenth century, fusing pseudo-classical divinities with *Rose*'s moral abstractions (Yates 1968:142).

Antiquarians of the eighteenth century and literary historians of the nineteenth and twentieth centuries rescued it from the obscurity into which it fell during the seventeenth century. The first complete English translation was published in 1900 by Frederick Startridge Ellis, a friend of literary figures and dealer in rare books. He gave a misleading and bowdlerized version of the poem, and with Victorian reticence refused to translate the conclusion. C. S. Lewis's *Allegory of Love* (1936) reevaluated *Rose*; his publication indicates the renewed interest in medieval allegory, or perhaps symbolist approaches in general, during the twentieth century. The enormously successful *Name of the Rose* by the twentieth-century semiotician Umberto Eco was inspired by *Rose* and its version of the world as symbol.

The Scholastic Rose:
Love, Reason, and the Principle of Plenitude

According to Alan Gunn (1952) and other modern commentators on *Rose*, the poem must be understood as an allegory, an extended description in which each part constitutes a particular doctrine or subject. The poem is less a narrative than a disputation, a representation of multiple points of view about love.

Charles Dahlberg (1971:10-11) calls attention to a change in literary style from Cicero's distinction between levels of decorum relegated to different subject matter, and Christian orators' methods of making everything sublime, the subject of revelation--a change that reflects the Augustinian integration of the corporeal with the intellectual. All expressions of human desire, from humble carnality to noble Godly love, are hierarchically related expressions of love according to the principle of plenitude. God's love was creative or generative, taking in all levels of existence. The expansiveness and self-transcendently of "the Good" is conveyed by two powerful metaphors that recurred for centuries: the chain and the series of mirrors in which God is reflected, sometimes dimly, in the phenomenal world. Arthur Lovejoy quotes Macrobius:

> Since, from the Supreme God Mind arises, and from Mind, Soul, and since this in turn creates all subsequent things and fills them all with life, and since this single radiance illumines all and is reflected in each, as a single face might be reflected in many mirrors placed in a series; and since all things follow in continuous succession, degenerating in sequence to the very bottom of the series, the attentive observer will discover a connection of parts, from the Supreme God down to the last dregs of things, mutually linked together and without break. And this is Homer's golden chain, which God, he says, bade hang down from heaven to earth. (1936:63)

According to Plato in the *Timaeus*, and to Plotinus in the Neoplatonic principle of emanations, God embodies the principle of Becoming. The universe is in the process of being filled with the numerous reflections of God whose nature is generative and fecund. Because of the principle of plenitude, the great chain of being must be completely filled; any gap implies chaos. Thus we find the strain toward encyclopedic completion of all topics--the acceptance of all biological forms, including those that we would consider today be miraculous monsters with eyes in their bellies; all the reflections of love in *The Romance of the Rose*, all expressions of vice in Dante's *Inferno*. Medieval men, longing for paradise as exiles desire a homeland (Fleming 1969:56), looked for all the manifestations of God in the world, no matter how dim were His reflections.

According to Dawson (1958:15), Europe has been continuously shaken and transformed throughout its history because its religious ideal (the Judeo-Christian tradition) is not the worship of "timeless and changeless perfection but a spirit that strives to incorporate itself in humanity and to change the world." As a manifestation of this, the "voracious hunger of the medieval doctors to relate all knowledge to the central fact of human and divine history" (Fleming 1969:90) incorporated all aspects of human life as a multi-dimensional allegory for the presence of the divine in human life. In this sense, carnal love and spiritual love were closely linked.

In lines 15135-15153, de Meun tells the reader that he is in a wood, reminiscent of the opening lines of *The Divine Comedy*--in effect, lost amidst love and its complexities. He declares that he is holding up a mirror to love to reflect "the true images of love's varied dance." Charles Dunn (1962:xxi) notes the importance of the ideas of Bernard Silvester of Tours. In *Universe of the World* (ca. 1145-53), Silvester expresses the concept that the Divine Mind created all things in a hierarchical system, within which the generative principle (Genius) conquers Death and averts the return of Chaos. Silvester's idea was developed by Alan de Lille who, in *Complaint of Nature*, opposed the idea that intercourse was evil. On behalf of Nature he condemned those who were derelict in their natural generative functions. God delegates the work of creation to Mind or Nature; Nature in turn has subordinate deputies, Venus and Cupid. Dante himself, in his description of the heavenly Rose of Paradise, is more graphic than contemporary readers might expect:

> Thou Virgin Mother, daughter of thy Son. . . .
> Within thy womb rekindled was the love,
> By heat of which in the eternal peace
> After such wise this flower has germinated.
>   *(Paradiso*, Canto 33, Lines 1, 7-9)

Sexuality meant something quite different in the thirteenth century than it does in the twentieth. Sex in all its physical, emotional, and symbolic manifestations was not a route to the netherworld of Freudian dynamics, but a route up the hierarchy of being to God and Reason. During the Middle Ages, the physical dimensions of human sexuality were perceived as secondary manifestations of a transcendent spiritual reality; the profane world was rooted in the sacred as a manifestation of all the images of God, no matter how darkly they were reflected in the mirror. For Freud and other heirs of Enlightenment thinking, spiritual realities were sanitized transmutations of animal necessity; the sacred was a transmuted version of the profane, images of a seething underworld processed through the rationalizing filters of ego in accordance with the restrictive, anti-id dictates of the superego. God, during the Middle Ages, was the creative, fecund source, and Reason was humanity's guide to a full and complete understanding of love. To Freud, the true lover was the uninhibited artist who could reach down into the unconscious. In the romantic vision, individuals had become gods, the id their divinity, and the dream was the royal road to truth (self-understanding).

The tradition of expressing the relationship between the soul and Ideas as one of intense love goes back to Plato; total union with the beloved is expressed in powerful sexual imagery, as in the passage, "it was the nature of the real lover of knowledge to strive emulously for true being . . . and the edge of his passion would not be blunted nor would his desire fail till he came into touch with . . . reality" (*Republic* VI, 490 a-b).

Often, in the medieval writings of John of the Cross, Teresa of Avila, Dante, and many anonymous ballads, the soul is portrayed as a female element in a mystical-sexual union with God that is overpowered, or even possibly raped, as expressed during the late sixteenth and seventeenth century by the poet-preacher, John Donne:

Batter my heart, three-personed God. . . .
Take me to you, imprison me, for I,
Except you enthrall me, never shall be free,
Nor ever chaste, except you ravish me.
(John Donne, "Holy Sonnets, 14," Lines 1, 12-14)

St. Paul's Epistle to the Romans introduces the exegetical method by which carnal is translated into spiritual love, old into new, providing a vocabulary that was useful to Dante, Chaucer, and Petrarch. From the time of St. Augustine, *amor* connoted both charity, God, and cupidity, Cupid. Lady Reason's praise of charity and warning against cupidity is the double lesson of love conveyed by the poem, and receives the greatest commentary in the margins of old manuscripts (Fleming 1969:103). The doctrine of plenitude, cited by Reason, puts sexual relations into the larger scheme of things. St. Augustine dealt with the question of sexual relations in paradise, arguing that the sexual organs were responsive to the rational will and were not evil if used properly. Sin is not coitus but the rejection of Reason. In this sense *Rose* is a morality play in which Everyman, the Foolish Lover, receives both good and bad counsel. Medieval allegories were not twentieth-century novels in which the omniscient author states his single, god-like position; they were full of different voices, all considered to be reflections or manifestations of God.

In the *Rose*, the Lover's desire for the rose is that of cupidity, love of an earthly object for its own sake rather than for the love of God. The examples provide ironic counterparts to the literary conventions of divine love. According to John Huizinga (1954:27), medieval doctrine saw the root of evil in pride and cupidity. Pride was the sin of a feudal and hierarchic age; because property was not liquid, power was inherent in the person and inspired religious awe. Grandeur was expressed in visible signs, was a symbolic sin. With the increased circulation of money, people could heap up wealth; tangible yellow gold haunted the imagination. Riches were direct and primitive, not weakened by the invisible accumulation of investment which capitalism, founded on credit, implies. The satisfaction of being rich was found in luxury, dissipation, and gross avarice (see Heer 1961:377).

The progression of imagery in the poem is like a version of the Fall: the overthrow of Reason and progressive involvement with sin. The ten commandments of Amours parody the Ten Commandments of the Bible. The mock religiosity of the Lover's quest is an aberration of the celestial pilgrimage, and becomes a carnal pilgrimage to the shrines of concupiscence. The final lines of the poem, "Straightaway it was day and I awoke," suggest the awakening of understanding as a result of the allegorical lesson. The Lover "wakes up" to the beginning of his dream which is a form of contemplation by which the dreamer progresses through the hierarchy of knowing. As he goes through the dream, he holds a mirror to the complexity of different points of view, and in the process gains in understanding. The dream is a bridge to knowledge. As a result of this allegorical journey, he "wakes up" to true knowledge, or at least, a higher form of knowledge than when he first fell asleep.

"Modern" Awakenings: A Comparison

A seventeenth-century Renaissance awakening scene is found in Pedro Calderon de la Barca's *Life's a Dream* (1636) that will be discussed in the next chapter. Sigismund, despite his love for Rosaura, conquers his desire in order to do what is right, even though he is unable to tell whether he is living in a dream or reality. The allegorical *Rose*, obviously used as a reference, has assumed a more humanistic, realistic, secularized version of virtue and human choice.

The image of the dreamer awakening at the end of *Rose* may also be contrasted with the conclusion of H. P. Lovecraft's twentieth-century *The Dream-Quest of Unknown Kadath* (1939). "Randolph Carter leaped shoutingly awake within his Boston room" after he had dreamed his way, like a shaman returning from a voyage to the underworld of his imagination, back into the "real" world: "and now there were re-made a waking world and an old cherished city to body and to justify these things" (Lovecraft 1970: 140). In the twentieth century, the "real world" is the familiar beauty of the phenomenal world. The kingdom of dreams is allied with the imagination. The gods of this world feel jealous that they did not create it, and seek to enter this world by capturing the dreamer who dreams them into existence: "for verily, they craved the weird loveliness of that which your fancy had fashioned, and vowed that henceforward no other spot should be their abode" (Lovecraft 1970: 130). Man is made in the image of God--has become God, a spiritual creator able to challenge the gods of the imagination. Humans as daimonic shamans go to the divine part of themselves to have discourse with and do battle with the gods. "You have dreamed too well, O wise arch-dreamer, for you have drawn dream's gods away from the world of all men's visions to that which is wholly yours; having builded out of your boyhood's small fancies a city more lovely than all the phantoms that have gone before." (Lovecraft 1970:131)

THE DIVINE COMEDY (LA COMMEDIA)

The Dantean Journey
versus the Instructional Allegory

Writers today refer to a "Dantean" pattern (Edel 1982:164), meaning a shamanistic descent to Hell and gradual emergence, a personal journey through madness, creativity, or depression in search of divine insight. This is a modern use of what was, in the fourteenth century, not a shamanic journey at all but a use of the allegorical dream vision conveying, as did Macrobius, support for the commonwealth and the social order. It was a medieval, instructional, encyclopaedic allegory of love. *The Divine Comedy* reflects the tradition of the allegorical writings from France and Germany, in particular *The Romance of the Rose*, and even some of their content; an anonymous thirteenth-century poem preceding *Comedy* divides Inferno into eight sections, each over 1,000 miles long, with ten gateways 100 miles apart, and volcanoes, seas, and lakes at each entrance. But although Dante belongs firmly to the tradition of the medieval allegorical dream vision, he stands apart. His allegory goes far beyond *Rose* in the density of its metaphors and, above all, in its vivid realism--shades of the Renaissance.

Dante Alighieri was born in Florence in 1265 to a family with some claims to nobility. In his youth he wrote love poems, and, in the Scholastic tradition of the *Rose*, combined courtly love with concepts of philosophic, spiritual, or divine love. The incarnation of divinity, as Divine Beauty or Divine Wisdom, for Dante was Beatrice Portinari, as the divine "Laura" was to Petrarch in the fourteenth century. In *Vita Nuova*, written when he was twenty-seven years old, he explains that all his poems had developed from his conception of Beatrice as a symbol of love, and in the last paragraph refers to a vision which he hopes will guide his studies so that eventually he may write "what never before has been said [in praise] of mortal woman."

In 1302 he was ousted from government by an opposing faction, was fined and exiled, and began his life as a wanderer. Eventually he became famous as a poet, wrote extensively about the historic problems of his age, especially the conflict between the Roman Catholic Church and the Holy Roman Empire, and was ultimately buried in Ravenna. Through his writings, he created a literary tongue based on the popular speech of Florence. The work of two later Florentine writers, Petrarch and Boccaccio, helped assure the supremacy of the Tuscan dialect as a literary language for all of Italy.

The Visual Vernacular
versus the Intellectual Classic

In 1300, when he was thirty-five years old, Dante began to write the work that eventually came to be known as *The Divine Comedy*. He called it a *Commedia* (Italian) or *Comedia* (Latin) because, in the classical definition expressed by Aristotle in *Poetics*, it dealt with a low-born rather than a noble person--in the Christian version, Everyman as opposed to saints. It also used popular language instead of Latin and was more realistic in its description than classical allegories (see Curtius 1953). The intent was not to inspire by divine life, as in the lives of the saints, but to instruct foolish, naive sinners. Forty years after Dante's death, Boccaccio described the work as "divine." The title *The Divine Comedy* did not appear as a frontispiece until the sixteenth century.

The same distinction between "high" and "low" modes of knowing in the Augustinian hierarchy (intellectual-classical vs. corporeal/vernacular-visual) is used to evaluate "good" as opposed to "bad" literature today. Dante's comedy was to the classics as the comic-book genre is to novels and other "serious" literature today. Comics are a visual vernacular form and *The Divine Comedy* provided illustrators, such as Gustave Dore, with a wealth of descriptions. As was the fate with Dante (and Chaucer), the comic book is being taken more seriously today than when it first appeared (Eisner 1990). Anthropologists have been known to interpret them as the symbolic vehicles of meaning in popular culture--or as a medieval Scholastic would say, allegorically.

Dante uses every traditional metaphor available to communicate the process by which Everyman (the morose, unhappy Dante) progresses to enlightenment: water barriers (*Rose*, interestingly enough, is set on the human rather than divine side of the river--a parody of the transcendent journey); woods and gardens; the dense physical heaviness of hell versus the incorporeal lightness of heaven; the dim, obscure light of hell compared to the overwhelmingly brilliant light of heaven; taking the narrow, difficult road; climbing mountains and ladders; and, in the final stage of ascent to paradise, taking the contemplative dream flight.   His starkly realistic descriptions of the tortures of hell print grim images on the imaginative powers of the soul--sufficient to frighten people into embracing the safety of salvation even if they are not convinced by the pale, transcendent truths of paradise that Dante tries but, in his own words, fails to describe--like the man described by Paul who was taken up to the third heaven.

Dante represents humankind, the Everyman-sinner who walks in the Wood of Worldliness, Error, or Sin, a common medieval metaphor (see Le Goff 1988 for a discussion of the role of the forest in the medieval imagination). He tries to climb the Mountain of Righteousness and is attacked by a leopard (Luxury), a lion (Pride), and a she-wolf (Greed). He is aided by Virgil, who represents Reason or Philosophy, and sometimes the Roman Empire. His guide to heavenly grace is Beatrice, who represents Revelation, Theology, or the Church. Like other medieval allegories, his work is an encyclopaedia of knowledge of the Middle Ages. Dante expounds philosophical, astronomical, physical, and theological theories. He describes the history of the Roman Empire as divinely ordained to prepare the world for Christianity; he describes medieval customs and institutions; he also makes historical judgments of his own by putting his enemies at various levels of hell.

In the tradition of the medieval allegorical dream vision of "awakening" via a dream, the action takes place between Good Friday (the Crucifixion) and Easter Sunday (the Resurrection), when he awakens. After seeing the consequences of sin and traversing the metaphors of enlightenment, Dante finally witnesses the apex of his dream vision: the heavenly rose.

In fashion then as of a snow-white rose
Displayed itself to me the saintly host,
Whom Christ in his own blood had made his bride.
(*Paradiso*, Canto 31, Lines 1-3)

BRIDGES TO THE RENAISSANCE:
PETRARCH, PIERS PLOWMAN, AND CHAUCER

Francesco di Petrarco: 1304-1374

Petrarch is sometimes identified as the founder of humanism, as inaugurator of the Renaissance in Italy, as someone who stood on the threshold of the Middle Ages imbued with a modern spirit. However, he differs very little from Dante in his orthodox religious beliefs, his respect for the Classical-Christian vision, and his synthesis of corporeal and intellectual levels of love. He was highly honored during his lifetime for continuing to develop, in passionate rhetoric and poetry, the vernacular Tuscan dialect that Dante had ennobled.

He was modern in his conception of Italy as a single nation unified by a common spirit, which he celebrated with odes even as he was busy acting as a go-between for the competitive tyrants of local city-states. He encouraged the collection of secular libraries and freed himself from the extreme allegorical form typical of the Middle Ages--although he wrote the allegorical *Trionfi* (Triumphs of Love, Chastity, Death, Fame, Time, and Divinity) and converted the object of his passionate love (the pseudonymous "Laura," presumably a married woman that he loved from afar for twenty-one years until she died of the plague in 1348) into an idealistic abstraction.

With regard to the doctrine of love I would place him midway between Dante and the earthy Boccaccio (*The Decameron*), based solely on his choice of classical quotes in his dream vision. When St. Augustine comes to him in his *secretum* (the "secret" dialogue of the Classical Age, in the form of a dream vision), he quotes Virgil: "Those who love, fabricate dreams for themselves" (Fleming 1984:160). I interpret this to mean that, like the seventeenth-century John Milton ("I waked, she fled, and day brought back my night"), he would sometimes prefer his sweetheart in the flesh--and if not, in a lusty Macrobian *insomnium*.

The Rise of the Modern Voice:
A Comparison of Piers Plowman and Chaucer

Piers Plowman: The Vision of William concerning Piers the Plowman, together with Vita de Do-wel, Do-bet, et Do-best, secundum Wit et Resoun was supposedly written sometime between 1362 and 1395 by a single author, William Langland (ca. 1332-1400). Although a contemporary of Chaucer, Langland belongs to the earlier allegorical tradition of the medieval dream vision, whereas Chaucer represents a new epistemological approach.

The poem is presumably based on an actual vision experienced by the author when he was about thirty years old, and begins with his falling asleep beside a stream in the Malvern hills and awakening to the vision. The poem exists in three forms. It is divided into four visions: Visio de Petro Plowman, Visio de Do-wel, Visio de Do-bet, and Visio de Do-best. The names are interpreted to mean Christ (Piers Plowman), and three personified actions: One who acts in a kind manner does well (Do-wel), one who teaches someone else to act kindly does better (Do-bet), and one who does both, who combines theory and practice, does best (Do-best). Highly critical of the Roman Catholic clergy--a prophetic voice of the Reformation--*Piers Plowman* resembles *The Romance of the Rose* in both its allegory and satire. It also resembles the later, seventeenth-century *Pilgrim's Progress: In the Similitude of a Dream*, the ascetic allegorical vision of an accomplished Reformation--the Rose purified and almost lifeless except for the passionate humility of its narrator.

According to M. B. Garber (1974), the medieval tradition of the dream vision culminated in England with Chaucer (A.D. 1340-1400). I suggest that he represents a good example of the cultural transition occurring between the Middle Ages and the Renaissance, a transition from medieval to early modern society. As a medievalist he was linked with classical traditions and was the first to translate the French *Roman de la Rose* into Middle English--*Romaunt of the Rose* (Luria 1982:24). Like Boccaccio and Dante, he too was ambivalent about his commitment to divine rather than secular love.

The son of a wealthy vintner, Chaucer was born in London. He mixes his English with Latin, French, and Italian. A relatively successful man of letters until late in life, he died in reduced circumstances in 1400.

His dream poems are minor compared with the *Canterbury Tales* and the *Troilus*, but they are major compared with other dream poems of the period, such as *Wynnere and Wastoure* and *The Parelement of the Thre Ages* (see Kittredge 1915 for a discussion of dream poems typical of the thirteenth to fifteenth centuries).

After translating *The Romance of the Rose*, he wrote *The Book of the Duchess*, an elegy for Blanche of Lancaster, wife of John of Gaunt (who during Chaucer's lifetime was a patron and friend). The protagonist of *The Book of the Duchess*, deep in melancholy, is an intellectual, who reads to lift his spirits. After reading the tale of Ceyx and Alcyone, in which a woman dies of despair, he has a dream about another despondent man, the Man in Black, who has played with Fortune, the tyrant of the mortal world if you accept her as such, and lost. The Man in Black refuses to repent, curses Fortune, and blames Death. Chaucer suggests that melancholy is self-imposed; the protagonist awakens from his dream unenlightened and not yet free from his depression.

In his next dream poem, *The House of Fame*, he was influenced by the encyclopaedic dream vision of *The Divine Comedy* and writings of Boccaccio, whose influence was felt particularly in the poem of betrayed love, *Troilus and Criseyde*. But instead of living in darkness, the protagonist, a poet who sings songs of love, lives in silence; and just as Dante went from dimness to light, the protagonist of *The House of Fame* is in quest of words. After an encyclopaedic perusal of the tidings of various sources (symbolized by the worldly house of good tidings, Fame, where airy tidings congregate--as in Andy Warhol's "fifteen minutes of fame"), he ends with a recognition of tidings that are not told and that correspond with the dumb, transcendent tidings of Paul's man who ascended to the third heaven.

Whereas *The Book of the Duchess* dealt with the allegory of Fortune, and *The House of Fame* with reputation, *The Parliament of Fowls* returns to the topic of *The Romance of the Rose*: Love. The poem includes a condensed version of the *Dream of Scipio*, and it is Scipio who conducts the narrator into a garden of Love, where sweet birds sing. The two goddesses of love are Venus, who with her son Cupid represents a love that is lascivious and disharmonious, the cacophonous Fowls of the title, and Nature. The figure of Nature is the agent of a loving God, full of joy and harmony. The formel-- the bird that is the object of love among the competing fowl--is told by Nature that she must make up her own mind; and the protagonist awakens from the dream with the choice as yet undecided.

The fourteenth century began with Boniface VIII's bull, *Unam Sanctam* (1302), a final and extreme statement of papal claims to authority over Christian society (Hollister 1973:237) that was to become increasingly out of touch with political reality. It was a time of the Black Death, when the great decline in population contributed to the breakdown of the feudal system and increased mobility of the population. Although modern English poetry is said to have begun with Chaucer, after the fourteenth century there was a major change in language and Chaucer's verses were not understood; he was not widely read until he was revived in the eighteenth century. He was more "modern" in the sense that Dante was more modern, having a more distinctive and individual vision rather than one didactically communal. Like the authors of *Rose*, he was a master of irony and satire; like Dante, he wrote in the vernacular while at the same time reflecting an encyclopaedic knowledge; but in his doubt and skepticism, keen observation, enjoyment of earthly delights, and distaste for hypocrisy, he may be linked with the realism of the Renaissance.

6

Learning to Cultivate One's Garden: Reason and Reality During the Renaissance

Dear love, for nothing less than thee
Would I have broke this happy dream;
It was a theme
For reason, much too strong for fantasy. . . .
Thou art so true that thoughts of thee suffice
To make dreams truths and fables histories.
    John Donne, "The Dream"

THE RENAISSANCE AS A MIDDLE AGE
BETWEEN THE MIDDLE AGES AND THE ENLIGHTENMENT

The Renaissance (French for "rebirth"--referring to the rebirth of classical thought after the "hiatus" of the "frozen" Middle Ages) emerged in Italy by the fourteenth century and reached its height in the fifteenth and sixteenth centuries. In the rest of Europe, the Renaissance is associated with the mid-fifteenth to the seventeenth centuries. It is usually identified as a time of individual expression, self-consciousness, and worldly experience; a time of emerging nation-states, the Age of Exploration, and revolution in commerce and science. So intent are scholars on embracing the "modern spirit" of the Renaissance and separating it from the Middle Ages that they often ignore how similar the two periods are. Both ages were intensely religious; the Classical/Christian synthesis continued (and, indeed, is still with us today);

and the rumbles of change that were to transform feudalism and fling European culture out across the oceans to the "New World" began long before 1492 (see Fernandez-Armesto 1987; Phillips 1988).

This chapter considers the Renaissance as a transition period between the Middle Ages and the Enlightenment, as a period within which the debate about what is real and the importance of reason to investigate reality was thrashed out. The debates of the Renaissance reflect changes in medieval ways of defining reality and presage conclusions reached and stated with conviction during the Enlightenment.

The Enlightenment, also called the Age of Reason and, in Germany, the *Aufklarung*, refers to the period between the late-seventeenth and late-eighteenth centuries in which thinkers such as Locke and Hume in Britain, and Diderot and Voltaire in France spoke out in clear, unambivalent voices against the blind authority of tradition and for a rational, and in most cases empirical, investigation of the phenomenal world. The world view of this period was secular and human-centered, with widespread belief in natural law and confidence in human reason to investigate empirically all aspects of human life--economic, political, social, and religious.

As the Renaissance segued, with epistemological complexity, into the Enlightenment, God became steadily depersonalized, secularized, and internalized in humans. In this humanistic framework, naturalistically run and empirically investigated, Reason retained its position as the major avenue to truth, thus necessitating the invention of the unconscious and the complex set of beliefs identified as the Romantic Movement in the late-eighteenth and nineteenth centuries.

CONTINUATION OF MEDIEVAL USES OF THE DREAM DURING THE RENAISSANCE

In the sixteenth century Dante's *Comedy* had become Divine, and in the pious, absolutist context of the Reformation, *Rose* had been declared naughty. But the dream continued to be used to conceptualize the manifestation of the divine in human life: as higher knowledge providing prophecy, as divine inspiration, and as an allegory of the human journey toward salvation. The prophetic dreams and the allegorical dream visions show little structural difference from their medieval counterparts, but inspiration takes on more secular connotations. This section provides examples of prophecy and allegory, comparing Milton's *Paradise Lost* with *The Inferno*--to hint at changes going on in the concept of inspiration, and concluding with a discussion of Calderon de la Barca's *Life's a Dream* as a Renaissance forum for discussion of reality.

Prophecy

Brian Hill (1967) provides numerous accounts from journals, books, personal recollection, and hearsay of prophetic dreams from the Renaissance. Cardinal Pietro Bembo (1470-1547) was warned by his mother through a dream to avoid a certain person who would wound him in his right hand; in a subsequent duel he fought with that particular man and was wounded in the second finger of the right hand. Sir Thomas White, Lord Mayor of London (1492-1567), founded a college at a site where three elms grow out of one root because he dreamed that he had done so. Nicholas Claude de Peiresc (1580-1637) dreamed about finding a gold medal of Julius Caesar in a goldsmith's shop for four crowns, and the dream came true. Oliver Cromwell (1599-1658) was told by a dream vision that he would be the greatest man in England, and Lady Hutchinson (1620-1671) was told by her mother that before she was born, the mother had dreamed that a star came into her hand, thus signifying that she would have a daughter of "some extraordinary eminency." The architect Christopher Wren (1632-1723) was cured of illness by a dream figure from Egypt that told him to eat dates. John Aubrey (1626-1697) reported the dream of Farmer Good: visited by a dead friend, Good was warned to stay in bed or he would die; he got up and died--at age eighty-four.

One of the most pathetic dreams reported by Hill is that of John Dee (1527-1608), an English mathematician and occultist who was accused of practicing sorcery against Queen Mary I, but was a favorite of Elizabeth I. He showed his practical talents in numerous ways--he was good at hydrographical and geographical description of newly discovered lands, and his calculations were used to adopt the Gregorian calendar in England. But he was best known for his interest in crystal-gazing, divination, and the occult, an interest that eventually led to his destruction. He joined forces and fortunes with Edward Kelly, who claimed to have discovered the alchemical secret of transmuting base metals into gold. They spent several years abroad and were patronized by various nobles and monarchs, who ultimately recognized them as frauds. Eventually Dee broke with Kelly and returned to England, where he died in disgrace and poverty. In his diary he recorded a dream that reflected his yearning for mystical knowledge: "This night I had the vision and shew of many bokes in my dreame, and among the rest was one great volume thik in large quarto, new printed, on the first page whereof as a title in great letters was printed *Notus in Judaea Deus*. Many other bokes. . . ." The dream evokes pathos because it reflects the driving passion during the Renaissance for knowledge and mastery of the phenomenal world and the ability of humans to deceive themselves with false patterns. The Renaissance was filled with alchemists who lost their fortunes, or others attempting to transform base metals into pure gold--a substance believed to lie higher on the mystical chain that organized the corporeal world. Many thinkers confused the exercise of reason with practical knowledge resulting from empirical investigation of the world.

The Reformation and the Allegorical Dream Vision:
Pilgrim's Progress

The allegorical dream vision, so rich and complex in the High Middle Ages, was adapted to the simplistic, pious formula of John Bunyan's (1628-1688) *Pilgrim's Progress: In the Similitude of a Dream*. Bunyan was a poor man with little education. Married at nineteen, he went through a number of years of religious struggle, and when his wife died in 1655 he began preaching as a Nonconformist preacher. During the Restoration he was imprisoned from 1660 to 1672 because he refused to stop preaching. He wrote a number of books during this period. *Pilgrim's Progress* was probably written during a later confinement of six months in 1675.

In 1672 Charles II suspended the laws against Nonconformists and Roman Catholics, and Bunyan became a successful preacher. The first edition of *Pilgrim* was published in 1678 and was enormously popular, especially among the New England Puritans, whose descendants took it with them in their movement westward.

In "The Author's Apology" at the beginning of the book he calls attention to his use of allegory to convey his message:

> The Prophets used much by Metaphors
> To set forth Truth . . .
> Am I afraid to say that Holy Writ,
> Which for its Stile and Phrase puts down all Wit,
> Is everywhere so full of all these things,
> Dark Figures, Allegories?. .
> Art thou for something rare and profitable?
> Wouldest thou see a Truth within a Fable?. .
> Would'st thou be in a Dream, and yet not sleep?
> (Lines 129-130, 133-136, 213-214, 229)

Pilgrim's Progress begins similarly to Dante's *Divine Comedy*: "As I walk'd through the wilderness of this world, I lighted on a certain place where was a Den, and I laid me down in that place to sleep; and as I slept, I dreamed a Dream. I dreamed, and behold I saw a Man cloathed with Rags."

The Man in Rags, like Chaucer's Man in Black, is the woeful protagonist of the tale. His name is Christian, and in his attempt to escape the Burden of the World and the fear that his City of Destruction, the World, will soon be "burned with fire from Heaven," he sets out on a journey to the Celestial City or Mount Zion, hindered and helped by a variety of personifications who speak a number of homilies. Evangelist tells him how to find the Wicket-gate, Christ); his neighbors Pliable and Obstinate turn back; he is helped out of the Slough of Despond by Help; he is misled by Mr. Worldly Wiseman and Mr. Legality, who lives in the town of Morality, and he is fired at with arrows from the nearby castle of Beelzebub.

In a passage that reflects the state of religion at the time, he passes through the Valley of Death, at the end of which is a Cave where the giants Pagan and Pope are said to live; he finds Pagan has been long dead, and Pope is ancient.

He meets Talkative, son of Say-well, who lives in Prating Row--"They say and do not"; "a saint abroad and a devil at home". He passes through a town called Vanity in which a Fair is being given, established five thousand years ago by Beelzebub, Apollyon, and Legion to waylay Pilgrims making their way to Zion. Because Christian and his traveling companion Faithful only want to buy the Truth, which is not for sale in Vanity Fair, they are imprisoned and put on trial by Judge Hategood. The witnesses against them are Envy, Superstition, and Pickthank. The jury, composed of Blind-man, No-good, Malice, Love-lust, Live-loose, Heady, High-mind, Enmity, Lyar, Cruelty, Hate-light, and Implacable, condemn them as Hereticks. Faithful is Scourged, Buffeted, Lanced, Stoned, and Burned at the Stake. Christian escapes and continues on his pilgrimage with Hopeful. In Doubting Castle of the giant Despair, they escape from the dungeon with the key of Promise. They are guided by Shepherds named Knowledge, Experience, Watchful, and Sincere past the Mountain of Error, Mount Caution, and the by-well to Hell. Like Dante, Christian finds the light of the Celestial City too intense for unaided human eye. They finally get to the City where the streets are paved with gold, are admitted, and given harps and crowns. Ignorance is turned away. "Then I saw that there was way to Hell even from the Gates of Heaven, as well as from the City of Destruction. So I awoke, and behold it was a Dream."

In a second part written later, Christian's wife, Christiana, and children go through their own pilgrimage to join him. The dream vision begins from a slightly different perspective: the author says he visited the region where Christian's wife and children lived, took Lodgings in a Wood nearby, and had another Dream in which he himself joins an old Gentleman who tells him what happened to the family. There are dreams within dreams--Christiana begins her pilgrimage because of a dream in which she sees her husband happily in heaven.

Inspiration

Like John Bunyan, the English poet John Milton (1608-1674) supported the Presbyterians in their attempts to reform the Church of England (but eventually broke with them). After the Restoration he was forced into hiding (Bunyan was in prison writing the many books that preceded *Pilgrim's Progress*). A biography of Milton (1698) was written by John Toland (1670-1722) whose life reflects the conflicts and controversies of this time. Toland was a Roman Catholic who converted to Protestantism, in 1694 tried to reconcile the scriptural claims of Christianity with the epistemology of John Locke (*Christianity Not Mysterious*), and in 1720 wrote a book that gave a name to the identification of God with impersonal nature (*Pantheism*).

Milton attributed his poetic inspiration to dreams (see Patterson 1931-1938) and also used medieval allegorical references to dreams and dream journeys. His language is dignified and ornate, full of biblical and classical allusions, allegorical representations, metaphors, puns, and rhetorical flourishes. In his fifth *Elegy* he is borne in dreams to Parnassus, the mountain ascended by Dante and numerous other medieval writers in search of divine understanding; his mind is freed from the body. In *Ad Patrem*, he attributes all his works to dreams in the shades of Parnassus. In *Paradise Lost* he solicits inspiration in the form of a dream. He is not so much a passive recipient of a vision as an active participant in a creative process. In Milton, the dream serves as a vehicle for recounting encyclopaedic truths, as it did in the Middle Ages, but it also serves as a symbol of his unique, distinctive, divine inspiration as a poet--shades of the Romantic Movement.

The difference between Milton and the Middle Ages is especially clear if we compare the Satan of his *Paradise Lost* with the Satan of Dante's *Inferno*. Milton wrote *Paradise Lost* and *Paradise Regained* to explain the presence of evil in the world and to "justify the ways of God to man." The characters are conveyed not as flat personifications but with humanistic sympathy, with an attempt to see things from their perspective. Many nineteenth-century critics, struck by the compelling, moving portrayal of Satan, said that he, rather than Adam or Christ, was the hero--a view typical of the Romantic Movement, which had respect for the creative, willful individual even if, and especially when, he broke the rules.

The Romance of the Almond:
The Use of the Dream to Explore What is Real

William Shakespeare (1564-1616), as one of the most outstanding playwrights of the Renaissance, is a tempting choice to use to examine conceptions of dream and reality during this time. Shakespeare uses dreams extensively in his plays. Garber (1974) does an admirable job of linking him with Classical traditions of Greece and Rome (the use of dream figures to develop the plot was a common technical device in Greek and Roman literature), with the medieval tradition of the dream vision, and with the native heritage of English folklore. Garber's subtitle, "From Metaphor to Metamorphosis," intended to reflect the classical journey toward enlightened wisdom up the Augustinian ladder that is conveyed by the allegorical dream vision, is also an apt expression of the change from the rigid hierarchy of the allegorical dream vision to the movement toward the Enlightenment that occurred during the Renaissance.

However, Shakespeare will figure here only indirectly, as an echo to his contemporary, Pedro Calderon de la Barca (1600-1681), whose play *Life's a Dream* (*La vida es un sueno*) may be interpreted as a multivocal dialogue on the nature of reality during the Renaissance. Calderon shares many of the same literary, philosophical, and dramatic conventions as Shakespeare, and German critics have equated them (see Sullivan 1983). But Calderon is less familiar to English-speaking audiences. His irony and passion over the debate about reality are more intensely expressed in *Life's a Dream* than in *Midsummer Night's Dream* or other dream plays by Shakespeare, and he has, since the beginning of the nineteenth century, been submerged in the Romantic swamps. I think that he deserves to be resurrected and placed in his historical context.

At the opening of the seventeenth century, the Dominican Giordano Bruno (1548-1600) was burned at the stake by the Inquisition for suggesting that our perception of the world is relative to the position in time and space from which we view it. Born in the same year that Bruno was burned at the stake, Calderon was educated at a Jesuit college, turned from theology to poetry and plays (he became a court poet in 1622), and in 1651 returned to the church as a Catholic priest, after which he wrote only *autos sacramentales*, allegorical celebrations of the Eucharist. He wrote more than one hundred plays, ranging from cloak-and-dagger to deeply philosophical, and was one of the most widely performed of all European dramatists in the seventeenth and eighteenth centuries. By the time he died in 1681, northern Europe was confirmed in its Protestantism, but his non-Catholic plays continued to be performed in Protestant countries.

Life's a Dream was first performed probably between 1631 and 1635, and first published in 1636. Rossini produced an opera based on the subject in 1814. According to Henry Sullivan (1983), it was first shown in German-speaking Europe in 1654 and was enormously popular in the years that followed. Lessing read it in 1750 and made sketches for a translation; it was translated from Spanish to German in 1803 and inspired Goethe, Grillparzer's *A Dream is Life*, and Wagner's *Tristan*. Edward Fitzgerald, the nineteenth-century English poet and translator of Omar Khayyam, wrote a dramatic poem that was a takeoff from Calderon called "Such Stuff as Dreams are Made of."

Life's a Dream was based on two Eastern stories known in Spain since the fourteenth century (Birch and Trend 1925): the "Sleeper Awakened" of the Arabian Nights in which a man is carried in his sleep to a palace, and the Buddhist parable of Barlaam and Josaphat (dramatized in Calderon's lifetime by the great playwright Lope de Vega) in which a prince is brought up in ignorance of the world and his place in it. The theme of awakening in *Life's a Dream* is the same medieval theme described earlier in this book, but with an Eastern twist introduced from Spain's Arabic past, and a Renaissance message.

The play opens on a craggy mountain in Poland where Polish prince Sigismund is being held prisoner by his father, Basilio, because of oneiric and astrological omens that he would be a tyrant. Sigismund is a Christ who will be "awakened" from death--but in this Renaissance version of awakening, he will arouse into a real world, not one dominated by silly prophecies.

Rosaura, a lady from Muscovy dressed as a man who is seeking the lover who betrayed her, is the Rose of *The Romance of the Rose* after the fall. Her lover Astolfo, Prince of Muscovy and nephew of Basilio, still loves the Rose but has come to Poland to woo his cousin Estrella and prevent a civil war that might erupt because Basilio, with Sigismund in prison, has no direct heir. Rosaura, accompanied by a wisecracking servant named Clarion, is the daughter of Clotaldo, Sigismund's jailer.

Basilio decides to free Sigismund because he thinks that the will might be more powerful than the influence of the planets. He plans to drug him, put him on the throne, and then if he shows signs of fulfilling the prophecy, drug him again and return him to prison. The plan is reminiscent of other experiments that were done during the Renaissance (for example, raising babies in isolation to determine their "natural" language) to discover what it meant to be human.

Sigismund is drugged with "opium, poppy, and henbane"--reminiscent of Prudence in de Lille's dream journey, who swooned and awoke to higher consciousness. But here what was a path to enlightenment has become a barrier to realistic understanding of the world. Basilio, seeking to minimize his son's disappointment if he must be returned to prison, instead creates an existential crisis for him. Through the play Sigismund wrestles with the question of what is real. In the text, dreaming appears to be both a metaphor for life in the phenomenal world, as opposed to the realm of the divine, and for unrealistic expectations about life in the phenomenal world. The former interpretation belongs to medieval idealism, the latter to empirical realism.

When Sigismund first awakes from the drugs and finds himself a king, he resolves his doubt with Cartesian simplicity: he knows that he is himself, and therefore he must be awake (Birch and Trend 1925:22). When Clotaldo reminds him to behave himself because he might find that his freedom is a dream, Sigismund is angered by his continuous harping on the subject. He threatens to kill Clotaldo--the ultimate empirical test of waking reality (see Birch and Trend 1925: 31-35). Medieval scholarship would not have been so committed to the factuality of the phenomenal world.

Because of his unruly behavior, Sigismund is drugged and returned to prison, and Clarion expresses the desire that he not awaken to his current situation. In medieval dream allegories, the awakening is the point of the dream; in *Life's a Dream*, one wakens to the ugly reality of life. By now, however, Sigismund has a new way to assess reality, one that affirms the medieval tradition of the Rose. He has fallen in love with Rosaura. As in medieval dream allegories, love remains the highest reality (Birch and Trend 1925: 46); but Sigismund's love is not the mystic, noncorporeal union with the divine, but a realistic love. Like Milton's "day brought back my night," or Donne's focus on a love so strong that it will reverse the natural order, Sigismund uses love as a touchstone of reality. Rosaura is more real as a "dream" than this awakened reality.

Sigismund gives his major speech on "life's a dream" at end of Act 2 (Birch and Trend 1925: 46-47). He says that only virtue endures; that life itself, from the pomp of kings to the chains of his current state, is an illusion, a dream. The meaning of awakening reflected in this speech is ambiguous. Do we awaken to a realistic conception of the world or to an enduring divine reality that lies beyond the phenomenal world? Do we awaken to wisdom by realizing that fame is illusory because, in the end, we all die? Calderon reminds us that there are several types of dreams, as Clarion, in Act 3, complains of nightmares caused by anxieties, lack of food, and indigestion.

The soldiers free Sigismund, saying that they are "awake" to their rights (Birch and Trend 1925: 52). Sigismund, wondering if he is dreaming again, refuses to be fortune's plaything, subject to illusions that vanish like almond blossoms that awake too soon and are scattered by the wind. Scene 1 of Act 3 ends with his decision to ignore the unanswerable question of whether his life is dream or reality and to get on with making decisions. In the end he does his civic duty and marries Estrella. Not every rocky road to realistic love has a Rose at the end of it.

In his final statement on dreams, he concludes that the only reality is the divine and its manifestation in good actions--a very medieval conclusion. However, unlike a medieval dream allegory, he raises Renaissance-like questions along his pilgrimage about the nature of reality, his affirmation of will, and the ability of the individual to create his own reality, questions that presage the Romantic Movement and probably explain his enthusiastic reception in nineteenth-century Germany. Sigismund is a Renaissance man still struggling to see through the dark glass of medieval theology. His symbol of awakening is not the eternal rose but the naturalistic almond struggling to bloom under confusing conditions.

THE SECULARIZATION OF THE DIVINE
AND THE QUEST FOR REALITY

Giordano Bruno, burned at the stake by the Inquisition in 1600, was one of many Renaissance thinkers dissatisfied with the idealistic formulations of medieval scholarship and reaching out for different ways of knowing the world. In the relativistic view that he espoused, there are as many different modes of viewing the world as there are possible positions. We cannot postulate absolute truth or any limit to the progress of knowledge. He considered himself no less religious than his judges; but the God responsible for this relativistic state of affairs was less like man and more like nature--a pantheistic formulation. Depersonalized, God becomes an infinite principle or cause whose laws may be discovered through reason.

What we are seeing is the beginnings of the secularization of the divine. As we saw in chapter 2, the change from the Homeric Age to the Classical Age was marked by an interiorization of the sacred other. The gods that had lived their own lives parallel to humankind were now linked, by means of an occult self, to humans. The dreams that had been figures sent from the world of gods to deliver messages had become a bridge between the human divine and the godly divine. Chapters 3, 4, and 5 demonstrated that in Neoplatonism, St. Augustine, Scholasticism, and the allegorical dream vision of the High Middle Ages, this umbilical cord of sacredness linked man to the One from whom all existence sprang. Dreams were proof of this linkage, a manifestation of the process by which the occult soul, through its imaginative-spiritual powers, achieved union with the Divine holy-whole. The invention of the occult soul started the process of the interiorization of the sacred other by which humans became, in effect, part god. This process continued into the Renaissance with the secularization of the divine.

Although the Renaissance is usually identified with humanism, specifically with the revival of the humanism of the Greeks and Romans, Renaissance humanism was different. "Humanism" means human-centered, with humans rather than God as the center of interpretation. In the Renaissance, this meant two things. On the one hand, Renaissance humanism celebrated the special, creative powers of the human individual--a continuation of the belief in an occult soul, except that the divine was becoming secularized. On the other hand, humanism implies a commitment to realism rather than idealism. The Homeric Greeks kept gods and humans separate. Gods existed, but they lived their own parallel lives, and dreams were their messengers. The life of man was down to earth, direct, practical, and to be lived and appreciated; the world was interesting, and humans should be known and understood as humans rather than gods. This aspect of Renaissance humanism was the same as Classical humanism: a commitment to the world as it was, an interest in perspective, lines on a real person's face in a portrait, morality as commitment to a social system rather than fulfillment of God's plan. Often these two aspects of humanism are confused. Calderon's *Life's a Dream* celebrates realism, but its greatest popularity was in Germany during the Romantic Movement (Sullivan 1983) because of the play's glorification of individual choice and will--the human as god.

The realism of the Renaissance was the small spark of paganism--not Classicism and Neoclassicism in its idealistic continuation of the classical-Christian integration, but Homeric paganism and its commitment to humans as humans separate from the gods. Realism does not bifurcate the self into true and untrue selves; it recognizes that to be human is to be many things ("half and half, and a little bit mixed" as Clarion says in *Life's a Dream*). In the mirror metaphor of the Middle Ages, all existence (reality) is a reflection of the One (the self) that is divided into true (the intellectual) and untrue (the corporeal) aspects. History is created through the process of ascending, via the untrue, to the true and thus achieving wholeness.

The scope of medieval learning was no less encyclopaedic than that of the "Renaissance Man," but during the Renaissance its focus shifted from glorification of the divine through exploration of the diverse corporeal to an enthusiastic interest in the workings of the phenomenal world for its own sake. Art retreated, often slowly (see Yates 1968), from the traditional allegory to a more realistic treatment of nature. Artists' subject matter indicated a greater interest in worldly life and unique human biography. In addition to portraying religious themes, artists explored portraiture, landscape, animal life, and historical subjects.

The Renaissance was intensely religious, whether in the perpetuation of medieval dogma, the evolution of Protestant reforms, or the quest for pagan mysteries (see Wind 1968). In the words of Maritain (1969:102), the Renaissance was preoccupied with mastery of nature and of the corporeal world, but Renaissance science was "a mystical covetousness of the earth." In discovering the natural laws that unified the arts and sciences, that produced the integrated diversity of the corporeal world, Renaissance thinkers were looking for the presence of the divine and trying to rationalize their commitment to the empirical world with theology. According to Leo Steinberg (1983), the Renaissance was preoccupied with incarnation theology--the fact that Christ had taken on the cloak of the human body, had assumed the identity of human nature. The manifestation of this incarnation theology, according to Steinberg, is a more naturalistic rendering of Christ in numerous examples of art from the mid-fifteenth to mid-sixteenth centuries--Christ has a penis, and everyone in the paintings seems to be looking at it. This naturalism did not challenge Christ's divinity but emphasized His humanity.

RENAISSANCE EPISTEMOLOGY

No longer satisfied with locating "reality" beyond the vast gulf that separated human flesh from the Divine Idea, Renaissance thinkers began to root for the real in the phenomenal, down-to-earth, empirical-consequences, warts-on-the-face, human world. Medieval Scholasticism, in its investigation of the relationship between reason and faith, took on the more secular intellectual orientation of humanism; it spawned methods of investigation that stimulated the rise of science and the glorification of the unique individual.

What is real? Augustine asked the same question when he considered Macrobius's categories of dreaming. What was a *visio*? What was "clear vision"? How did humans see and know reality? In the Classical-Christian synthesis, the "knowing" of the body produced trivial and insubstantial dreams, whereas the "knowing" of the soul produced divine dreams that reflected participation with *Nous*. The epistemology of the Renaissance continued this pattern, except that, with Descartes, it placed responsibility for knowing truth not in the hands of external agents such as angels and demons (by whom one was inspired or misled), but in the human thinker. The human must develop methods of thinking, apply standards of doubt, and come to conclusions not on the basis of faith but on whether the standards of reason have been met. In this context, dreams have no role; they are illusory and do not meet the canons of intellect. On the other hand, said Leibniz, perhaps there is a continuation of consciousness from the active meditations of conscious thought to the less active manifestations of the soul during sleep. Descartes separated the mind from the body, assigning dreams, illusions, sensory experience, and emotions to the body; the mind interacted with the body through the pineal gland. Leibniz created a parallel system of mind and body, each surrounded by "monads" that reverberated to each other in sympathetic harmony. Spinoza did not separate mind and body and developed a relativistic definition of "goodness" that depended on pleasure, but gave primacy to reason as the ultimate source of power and happiness. The following sections develop and explore some of these ideas, comparing and contrasting the Renaissance use of dreams with medieval and modern uses.

Descartes's Dream

I am . . . a real thing, and really existent; but what thing? . . . a thinking thing. (Descartes in Veitch 1960:121)

The Rationalism of Descartes, Spinoza, and Leibniz form a bridge between the concept of reason as used in the Middle Ages and the empiricism of John Locke and modern science. Descartes is often hailed as the founder of modern philosophy and the scientific method. It is ironic that he obtained his insight for his life's work not from the exercise of conscious intellect, but from a dream.

Rene Descartes (1596-1650) was a French philosopher, scientist, and mathematician who was educated at a Jesuit college and graduated in law. At the age of twenty-three, excited after a conversation with a friend, he fell into a restless sleep and had a dream (or three dreams, interpreted as one) that he recorded in his journal on 10 November, 1619. In the first dream, a wind blew around him on his way to church, which he later interpreted as an evil genius. Someone told him that a friend of his wanted to give him a melon, which he interpreted to mean love of solitude. He woke up in pain, turned over, and prayed to God for protection. His second dream was terrifying, and a loud noise awoke him to a room filled with sparks--remorse for sins committed during his life. In the third dream, he saw a dictionary, signifying all the sciences, and a *Corpus poetarum*, symbolic of Philosophy and Wisdom linked together, open to a passage from Ausonius, "What path shall I follow in life?" Verses handed to him included the phrase, "*Est et Non*," the "Yes and No" of Pythagoras, representing truth and falsity in human achievements. He woke up convinced that he had received a supernatural revelation-- warnings about his past life in the first two dreams, and a prophecy about his future mission to create an infallible system of knowledge that resolved issues about the relationship between human reason, faith, and reality. The meditations of November 1619 to March 1620 that followed his dream constitute the basis of Cartesian philosophy.

Descartes's dream has been discussed and analyzed for over three hundred years. His biographers debated whether it was a real dream or a vision, and whether it should be included in a description of his life. Enlightenment thinkers were both amused and outraged that the foundations of rational thought and scientific method should be the by-product of a fatigued and overexcited brain, a "cerebral episode" as Comte referred to it, interpreted as divine prophecy. Freud analyzed Descartes's dream (see Fliess 1953:118) but concluded that he needed Descartes's associations to the contents, especially the melon. Modern philosophers, such as Maritain (1969), psychologists, and literary critics use the dream as an opening for their respective topics.

Descartes was trained in the diverse theories of Scholasticism and found them contradictory and confusing, the cause of heresy and discord within the Church. He adopted the philosophical position that he would doubt everything until he was convinced otherwise. His attempt to find a foundation of knowledge in the study of "himself and the great book of the world, from nature and the observation of man" (*Discourse on Method*) led him to a method of arriving at logical conclusions, beginning with the proposition "I think therefore I exist."

In *Meditations*, Descartes makes the Augustinian distinction between knowing by the senses, knowing by the imagination, and knowing by the intellect (Veitch 1960:127). The conscious thought by which he arrives at the fact and necessity of his existence is the operation of the intellect. The wax that hangs in the beehive, is molded in the hand, and is finally melted in the fire can be known not by the senses (after all, the sensory experience of the wax is continuously changing under changing conditions) but through the rational exercise of conscious thought that arrives at the idea of wax. Only conscious thought can provide true ideas; the activity of the imagination can only lead to error--as he states in the following comment on images and dreams:

> the knowledge of my existence . . . is not dependent on any of the things I can feign in imagination . . . the phrase itself, I frame an image, reminds me of my error; for I should in truth frame one if I were to imagine myself to be anything, since to imagine is nothing more than to contemplate the figure or image of a corporeal thing; but I already know that I exist, and it is possible at the same time that all those images, and in general all that relates to the nature of body, are merely dreams (or chimeras) . . . . And, therefore, I know that nothing of all that I can embrace in imagination belongs to the knowledge which I have of myself, and that there is need to recall with the utmost care the mind from this mode of thinking, that it may be able to know its own nature with perfect distinctness. (Veitch 1960:121-122)

Dreams (his own dream notwithstanding) are not sources of knowledge, because knowledge can come only through the exercise of the intellect, which occurs only during conscious thought (also see Dunlop 1977).

His book *Traite des passions d l'ame* (1649) argued that emotions are physiologically based and can be disciplined by restraining their physical expression. Descartes said that mind and body were separate substances that interacted in the pineal gland, thus posing a problem of interactionalism that was dealt with by many philosophers. For example, Leibniz resolved the problem with sympathetically vibrating monads, and Malebranche, in the medievalist doctrine of occasionalism, argued that the immaterial does not ever interact with the material, and that finite things lack active power; God is the final cause. Today mind is considered by neurophysiologists to be an epiphenomenon of electrochemical processes, but debates about the ghost in the machine and expressions of awe and wonder over such a relationship (rather than an acceptance of this arrangement as "natural") reflect this centuries-old dualism.

Descartes began a systematic examination of the basis of his belief that something was true. Because dreams, sensory illusions, and false memories can appear to be true but are false, he concluded that all beliefs about the self and the world are suspect. Only the act of doubt itself is certain. To doubt is to think; to think is to exist. By an act of doubt, one constructs the external world.

Although the ability to doubt and to think comes from God, and the world of thought corresponds to the real world only because of the veracity of God, Descartes has taken the proof of reality out of God's hand and into a method of thinking. Theology has been separated from science; reason as practiced according to Cartesian methods no longer needs God or faith to know truth. The Admirable Science has become Science as we think about it today--a unified system of understanding, a powerful tool for breaking the crust of the unknown in all aspects of life.

Because this method is based on simple, clear truths, innate ideas that everyone has, science is accessible to everyone. It is not based on the complex and contradictory messages of the senses, but on universal, common ideas. From these simple ideas an entire world can be constructed through deduction, and it is theoretically possible to know everything. The original title of his *Discourse on Method* (1637) was *Project of a Universal Science Destined to Raise our Nature to its Highest Degree of Perfection*, and it included essays on everything from algebra to meteors in order to illustrate the universal science, the "positive" science that would integrate all knowledge. Descartes himself believed that it was possible for him to understand the workings of the body and thereby live forever (he died of pneumonia at age fifty-four). The optimism of Cartesian rationalism contained the hubris of the Enlightenment: the conviction that humans could mold the world to their rational conclusions through social movements, utopias, and the systematic development of science to interpret, predict, and control nature. The literary genre of science fiction originates, I believe, in the exploration of the dangers and temptations of this hubris, starting with books such as Mary Shelley's *Frankenstein* and Robert Louis Stevenson's *Dr. Jekyll and Mr. Hyde*. Also, the genre may be linked with earlier books that warned of the dangers of lusting after secular learning--*Doctor Faustus* by Christopher Marlowe (1564-1593) and *Faust* by Johann Wolfgang von Goethe (1749-1832).

Rationalism versus Irrationalism

Rationalism (from the Latin, "belonging to reason") has several meanings in modern usage. Loosely used, it implies confidence in the existence of an orderly universe and confidence in the mind's ability to detect this order, a confidence that can be traced to Descartes's method of applying Reason rather than faith and invocation of authorities to the development of a universal science. In this general sense, it is allied with science and the empirical investigation of the world to arrive at the laws by which nature appears to work and is opposed to *irrationalism*, which denies order or the ability of the mind to detect its coherence. The challenge to reason that occurred among the Romantics was based on this approach; they did not disagree with the rationalists that truth lay in the mind of the individual, but they placed their trust (or their despair) in the operation of the will, emotions, or the unconscious--to which dreams were a royal road. Thus Freud was both an empirical rationalist looking for patterns in nature and a romantic who placed the locus of reality not in reason but in the emotional unconscious.

In the Romantic dream poetry of Charles Baudelaire (1821-1867), classical symbols are combined with existential despair in his conviction that beauty and corruption are inseparable. The world, he says, is not orderly but full of chaos, and the only order and beauty possible exists in our irrational dreams.

Idealism versus Empiricism

More precisely used, the term Rationalism implies that reason alone, unaided by experience, can arrive at basic truths about the world. In this sense it is allied with the medieval doctrine of innate ideas--*idealism* opposed to *empiricism*. One must distrust the deceitful data from the senses and deduce truth about the world from "self-evident" premises. Dreams, in this context, are illusory. As Shakespeare's MacBeth said:

> Is this a dagger . . .
> Art thou not, fatal vision, sensible
> to feeling as to sight? or art thou but
> A dagger of the mind, a false creation,
> Proceeding from the heat-oppressed brain?
> (Shakespeare, *MacBeth*, Act II, Lines 33, 36-39)

Or, as the Chinese proverb asks: "Am I a human dreaming about being a butterfly, or a butterfly dreaming about being a human?"

Cartesian Rationalism sowed the seeds of later forms of Idealism. Idealism refers generally to the belief that ideas and ideals are products of the mind, in contrast with the world as perceived through the senses. In philosophy, the term refers to the idea that all objects in nature and experience are representations of the mind or a higher order of existence. The Idealist who dominated Classical and Medieval times was, of course, Plato, with his world of shadows deriving from Ideal Forms or Archetypes. Some modern idealists give an independent reality to causal principles separate from that which can be investigated empirically--such as Kant and the neo-Kantians; and Hegel's "objective idealism" argues that reality is a creation of the mind. The placement of superhuman mental activity or spiritual quality in the human (part of the process of the secularization of the divine) is an important aspect of the Romantic Movement.

The methods and assumptions of empirical epistemology were initially laid out by John Locke (1632-1704) who, in his *Essay Concerning Human Understanding* (1690), denied that innate ideas exist. The mind is a *tabula rasa*, a blank slate, and must acquire knowledge through experience. Experience comes through sensation and through reflection; all ideas may be traced back to experience. The limitation to his emphasis on ideas was pointed out by George Berkeley: If the only way we can know the world is through ideas, how do we know that the world exists?

The idealistic views of Rationalism fell into decline not through logical argument but primarily because the "science" developed from its premises (monadism, aethers, the pineal gland as a kind of mystical third eye) was defective. Knowledge of the workings of the world could be effectively gained not by thinking about the world, but through empirical investigation of it. Some of the debates, and implications of these debates for later formulations, are explored below.

Descartes rejected both dreams and sensory experience as reliable sources of knowledge; he separated mind and body and said that only the intellect, operating in conscious thought, could arrive at truth. Gottfried Wilhelm Leibniz (1646-1716), on the other hand, argued that all ideas, even those produced by sensory experience and those produced by the imagination, are produced by the soul and are innate. For example, in a takeoff from Locke's *Essay Concerning Human Understanding*, which was entitled *New Essays Concerning Human Understanding* and published in 1765 after the death of both Locke in 1704 and Leibniz in 1716, Leibniz, in the guise of "Theophilus," argues that perceptions occur in sleep that are not noticed or remembered. "We think of many things at a time, but we attend only to the thoughts which are most distinct, and that process cannot go on otherwise, for if we should attend to all, we would have to think attentively of an infinite number of things at the same time." The soul, because it is in close harmony with the body which is always active with the circulation of the blood, etc., is also in constant motion, even if we are not always aware of this motion. This view of dreams reflects Leibniz's attempt to salvage theology in an increasingly secular world. The universe is an integrated whole in which all parts relate, the result of a divine plan, and is the best of all possible worlds (a medieval concept satirized by Voltaire in *Candide*). The ultimate constituents of the universe are monads, simple substances incapable of action but whose apparent interaction is due to preestablished harmony. As in the medieval chain of being, "Nature makes no leaps." Monads are arranged in an infinitely ascending scale. All monads have perception--consciousness; only rational monads have apperception--self-consciousness.

Leibniz's speculations about dreams demonstrate distinctive features of Renaissance thinking: proof not by appeal to authority but by the application of a logical, rational method; and an attempt to come to terms with empirical reality. Unlike Descartes, he accepted that sensory experience and dreams are forms of conscious activity (sensory perception, imagination, and intellect differ only in the correctness or error of their calculations), and he tried to integrate medieval theology with a pseudo-empirical model. Body and soul were surrounded by monads that can exert an influence on each other without actually being in contact. He distinguished between truths of reason (resting on the principle of identity or contradiction--the old Aristotelian A/Null-A logic) and truths of fact (resting on the principle of sufficient reason or reality).

Leibniz was a philosopher, diplomat, and mathematician best known today for his discovery of the principles of differential and integral calculus. Christian von Wolff popularized his ideas in the eighteenth century, and in the twentieth century Leibniz has been identified as the founder of symbolic logic because he suggested that thinking could be reduced to universal symbols, or primal cognitions (like Descartes's "simple ideas"), that were then combined in more complex patterns (an idea that from his point of view revealed the workings of a divine, integrated plan that permeated the universe).

Voltaire (1694-1778), a French philosopher, scientist, and author, satirized the idealistic optimism of Leibniz and at the end of *Candide* suggested the common-sense advice that instead of speculating about unanswerable questions, we should "cultivate our gardens." He was both religious and skeptical, opposed to the pantheism of Toland and the materialism of Helvetius and Holvach, yet tentative in his expressions of belief ("If God did not exist, he would have to be invented"). Influenced by Locke and Montaigne, he espoused a practical philosophy and contributed greatly to the popularization of science. His thoughts are those of a religious person recognizing the usefulness of empirical investigation; he has not yet assumed the extreme optimism of Enlightenment thinkers who are convinced that they can remake the world. He would agree more with Montaigne than with Whitman in the passages below:

I seldome dreame; when I doe, it is of extravagant things and chymeras, commonly, produced of pleasant conceits, rather ridiculous than sorrowfull.

Michel de Montaigne (1533-1592)

I dream'd in a dream I saw a city invincible to the attacks of
the whole of the rest of the earth.
I dreamed this was the new city of Friends,
Nothing was greater there than the quality of robust love, it led the
rest,
It was seen every hour in the actions of the men of that city,
And in all their looks and works.

Walt Whitman (1819-1892)

Voltaire and Denis Diderot (1713-1784) were central players in the drama
of the Enlightenment. As editor of the *Encyclopedie*, Diderot enlisted nearly
all of the important French writers of the Enlightenment. Unlike Leibniz, he
was not concerned with preserving theological idealism (an avowed materialist, he influenced the materialism of Holvach and Helvetius); but like Leibniz, he thought that all impressions received by the senses are preserved,
even though we may not be conscious of this memory.

In the empiricist epistemology of John Locke, ideas are constructed from
sense impressions. When we reflect on these ideas, we do so through a chain
of association. Sometimes an experience triggers an associative process that
brings forgotten experiences to light. In an article, *"Reve,"* in the *Encyclopedie*, Diderot suggested that dreams are associations of ideas in involuntary
memory, especially those ideas that made their strongest impression on us
during the day.

To Diderot, such chains and complexes of associations were insignificant.
Dreams were partial and confused versions of normal thought processes, not
royal roads to Freud's enlightened unconscious. But this conception of
thought establishes a "layer-cake model of the psyche" (see Porter 1979) that
was mined by the Romantic Movement and ultimately encapsulated in a brilliant synthesis of Western cultural themes by Sigmund Freud.

Spinoza and Freud:
The Motor for the Machine

Benedictus de Spinoza (1632-77) was influenced by Scholastic theology,
Giordano Bruno, Rene Descartes, and Thomas Hobbes. Like Decartes and
Gottfried Wilhelm von Leibniz, he demonstrated an intensely mathematical
appreciation of the universe. Truth, like geometry, follows from first principles accessible and evident to the mind. Unlike Descartes and Leibniz, he
did not distinguish between mind and body, or between ideas and the physical universe--which he saw as two aspects of a single substance: God or, in
the same pantheistic genre as Bruno, depersonalized Nature.

Unlike Descartes and Leibniz, who considered sensory data to be either an interference with or a low form of reason, his deductive reasoning did not dispense with empirical observation. Like Leibniz, Spinoza agreed that "goodness" is defined by what gives pleasure; but he took a more relativistic path than Leibniz. Leibniz suggested, like Plato, that the soul's pursuit of reason brings the greatest pleasure, whereas Spinoza observed that since there are many different things that give people pleasure, there must be different types of "good." Spinoza appreciated the ideas of Hobbes, who said that all men have a drive for self-preservation by which they seek to maintain the power of their being. Thus virtue, what is defined as "good," is the same thing as power (Machiavelli would have appreciated his argument), and power comes from knowing, and doing, what is necessary. A powerful, or virtuous, man acts because he understands why he must, whereas other men act because they cannot help themselves. Hobbes said that humans want to satisfy as many desires as possible, and he emphasized the importance of repression for social order. Spinoza, because he thought that reason, through understanding, could conquer and control desire, stressed freedom, especially freedom of inquiry.

Like Freud, Spinoza argued that knowledge of one's nature confers power and freedom; bondage consists in being moved by causes that we do not understand. The difference between Freud and Spinoza is that Spinoza, reflecting the rationalist heritage, gives priority to reason to sort out the "confusion of ideas" that binds us, whereas Freud leaves reason behind (his reason, Ego, is allied with the learning theory of Locke and the social epistemology of Durkheim, placing the locus of knowledge in society, the Superego) and goes to the emotional pits of unreason in quest of knowledge.

Plato said that the philosopher, being trained in the powers of reason, was the best candidate to lead the Republic. In the same way, Spinoza confers power on his philosopher, and presages the cult of the Superman in German idealism. Rather than "I think therefore I exist," Spinoza's dictum could easily be, "I think therefore I act." He equated the will to action not with id or passion but with ideas themselves.

Descartes assumed responsibility for creating the world through thought; Spinoza gave credit to the Will as the source of motivation for Reason to act; Freud returned Reason to the passive status conferred on it by medievalists and occasionalists (God as final cause), identifying Will with seething, irrational passions (Hobbes's self-preserving lust for pleasure and power) to which the true self, the rational ego, must go for a full understanding. Freud's quest to understand human behavior is rooted in the empiricist's desire to investigate, to apply the principles of science to an explanation of reality; but the structure of his system reflects an ongoing Western cultural system.

7

The Romance of the Mushroom: Awakening in the Garden of Divine Garbage

The dream emerges "like a mushroom out of its mycelium." Each dream has a "navel," a "spot where it reaches down into the unknown. . . . a tangle of dream-thoughts which cannot be unravelled."

Sigmund Freud, *The Interpretation of Dreams*

When Descartes clobbered Scholastic authority over the head with doubt and took hold of the reins of Reason, he did three things: He validated the importance of knowing the empirical world; he continued the process of secularizing the divine and having humanity replace God as creative force; and, with his absolutistic concept of Reason, he necessitated the invention of the unconscious. Both the rise of science and the Romantic Movement may be understood in these terms.

Scientific method by itself is a means of investigating the empirical world; it is a tool with eminently practical consequences, and is validated by the falsifiability of its hypotheses--that is, its inspired guesses can be tested. Its purpose is to investigate things as they are--as objects--rather than as figments of our infatuation, or how we want them to be. People using the scientific method usually think of their findings as universal, and not confined by cultural parameters.

Nevertheless, the entire framework of science rests upon implicit cultural assumptions: that a phenomenal world exists, that it is important to investigate it, and that it is possible to investigate it. Such assumptions were certainly not self-evident to people during the Middle Ages, and there are those who challenge them today. The author of *Zen and the Art of Motorcycle Maintenance*, Robert M. Pirsig, observed that the more he knew about the world, the less he knew; scientific method seemed to him to generate an increasing, rather than decreasing, number of questions.

The Renaissance represents a transition from the divine-centered Middle Ages to Enlightenment commitment to the phenomenal world as a significant object of knowing and a shift in creative knowing from God to humans. The artist who depicted Christ with a penis and a naturalistically rendered audience departed dramatically from the medieval artist whose anonymous worshippers gazed with meditative sameness at heaven. Such artists share with later chemists, physiologists, and engineers, as well as with the Romantics, a belief in their own power of vision. The passive vessels of the Middle Ages whose sole use of their occult soul was to witness and give praise to divine creativity were now contributing to the creation of the world. In the Judeo-Christian tradition, history was a manifestation of divine will; but as God was moved off the center stage and into the wings, humans usurped will and interiorized the divine. The divine became secular, but it was still there: The creative force that the exclusively defined Reason proved to be too limiting a vessel to hold. The Romantics, dissatisfied with its limitations, discovered Unreason, allied madness and creativity, and in a complicated set of formulations (Will, Imagination, the Heart, Organ of Sensibility, multiple sets of nerves, etc.) presaged the invention of the unconscious. Freud's *Interpretation of Dreams* was a dramatic synthesis of all these traditions: It validated the epistemological structure of the Judeo-Christian tradition, invented a garden of divine garbage for the Romantics, and validated the framework of science. It also created the quintessential shamanic hero for the twentieth century--the psychiatrist.

ESTABLISHING THE LIMITS OF REASON

In taking up the Cartesian challenge, both the empiricists and the idealists set out to sketch and establish the boundaries of their methods and soon found that there were limits to what they could do. Instead of recreating the world, they built tiny islands.

David Hume (1711-1776) took Locke's empiricism to extremes, breaking down events into miniscule sensory experiences contiguous in time and space. One assumed causal relationships only because events were habitually associated with each other. Causality had become association; there was no basis for knowing whether the future would repeat the past.

Immanuel Kant (1724-1804) synthesized Hume and Leibniz in the *Critique of Pure Reason* (1781), a book that clearly demarcated phenomena, things knowable through sensory experience, from noumena, things unknowable but thinkable by reason. What had once been *nooumenon* in ancient Greek (a thing being perceived, derived from *noein*, to perceive) became that which can be the object only of a purely intellectual, nonsensory intuition. Instead of using one's *nous* to perceive God in the world, one cultivates the phenomenal garden, from which God (as knowable) has been excluded.

In 1766 Kant published *Dreams of a Spirit-Seer: Illustrated by Dreams of Metaphysics*, which is notable for its critique of the occult spiritualism that was popular during this time, in particular the apocalyptic mysticism of Emanuel Swedenborg (1688-1772). Swedenborg claimed to have received direct communication with the spirit world through dreams, and to have been told of the second coming of Christ. In a biography of Swedenborg published in 1868 by William White (see Almansi and Beguin 1986:281-282), Swedenborg says that his revelations began after he ate voraciously, saw his room swarm with hideous reptiles, and was told by a Man not to eat so much. Kant used Swedenborg's claims to discuss the limits of pure reason and its inability to know the spiritual realm in the same way that we know the empirical world. He warned against believing that one can directly experience of anything other than the empirical, phenomenal world: "The land of shadows is the paradise of dreamers. Here they find an unlimited country where they may build their houses *ad libitum*. Hypochondriac vapours, nursery tales, and monastic miracles provide them with ample building material" (Kant 1900:37). He ended with *Candide*'s wisdom, "Let us look after our happiness, go into the garden, and work" (Kant 1900:122).

It is symptomatic of the twentieth century that Kant's book was reissued (for example, Kant 1900--the same year that Freud's *Interpretation of Dreams* was published) and used to promote Swedenborgianism, a mystical cult that was founded after Swedenborg's death in 1772. The following quote from the psychiatrist J. Hillman's *The Dream and the Underworld* indicates that psychiatry has reconquered the land excluded by Kant: "The basic bedtime story of our culture is that to sleep is to dream and to dream is to enter the House of the Lord of the Dead where our complexes lie in wait. We do not go gentle into that good night" (Hillman 1979:34).

The dream of G. C. Lichtenberg (Mautner and Hatfield 1959) reflects an Enlightenment thinker's awareness of the limits of Reason. Lichtenberg (1742-1799) was a professor of math and astronomy who admired Kant, was respected for his empirical methods and cosmopolitan, humane aphorisms, and distrusted the unrestrained emotionalism of Germany at that time. Around the time of the American Revolution he visited and praised the British for their common sense (*Letters from England*, 1776-1778).

Lichtenberg dreamed that as he was soaring through the sky, he met God who gave him a bluish-green ball to investigate. He used every method of science at his command--he measured with instruments and tested with chemicals to understand the object that God had given him. When he was done, God told him he had studied the earth; and that in the process, he had wiped away the seas on a napkin, cut away Switzerland and the finest part of Sicily, and--oh yes, the speck of dust in his eye was a mountain.

God then handed him a book. In his dream, Lichtenberg realized that if he applied the same chemical tests, he would end up only with rags and printer's ink, but not with understanding. He woke up greatly moved by his dream.

On the other side of the Atlantic, Benjamin Rush, one of the signers of the Declaration of Independence and often called the father of American psychiatry, was having a similar dream. In 1785, during a period of national optimism, Rush dreamed that a great crowd was surging around Christ Church in Philadelphia (Edel 1982:119). A man had climbed the steeple and was sitting on the ball just below the weather vane. When Rush asked what was happening, his friend told him that the man had just discovered that he could control the weather. He held a trident in his hand like Neptune and flourished it as he shouted his commands at the sky. But Nature refused to comply with his commands, and the man sank into a deep depression. Rush told his friend that the man was mad. At this moment, a messenger dressed like Mercury descended from the steeple carrying a banner on which was inscribed *"De te fabula narratur"* ("About you a story is being told"). Rush woke up, realizing that the mad man wielding the trident and presuming to control the weather was himself.

In another dream (Edel 1982:121), Rush dreamed that he was elected president of the United States. At first declining the honor, he realized that if he accepted, he would have the opportunity to demolish drunkenness. But after he became president and passed prohibition, the country revolted. A stranger told him that America would not submit to his "Empire of Reason." Rush ordered him out and then woke up in anger and relief.

Like Lichtenberg, Rush was an Enlightenment thinker aware of the limits of Reason, as well as the dangers of scientific hubris.

THE ROMANTIC REACTION TO THE LIMITS OF REASON

Romanticism is usually described as a philosophical revolt against Rationalism, an exultation of the senses and emotion over Reason and intellect, and the Romantic imagination as a quasi-religious mode of perceiving ultimate truths (Bowra 1949; Benziger 1962; Colville 1970; Abrams 1953, 1971).

A Rationalist could starve to death on the mathematically lean theorems of Cartesian method, Humean skepticism, or Leibnizian monads; and although Spinoza recognized that values are defined by what gives pleasure, he believed that Reason could conquer desire. The reality that the Rationalists, both empiricists and idealists, worked to create proved rather anemic, limited in scope, and, as a system for generating a world, sterile. No matter how interesting, uplifting, or stimulating these readings are, they read, ultimately, like *Pilgrim's Progress*; they do not speak to the whole of the human condition. One yearns, after a while, for a hint of melancholy, a spark of maniacal laughter, a poetic ode to death and doubt; a flash of multivocal insight, a glimpse of chaos.

Now that humans were rooted in the corporeal world, stuck in the garden of phenomena, it was time not only to cultivate it, but to investigate its parameters. To use a more medieval metaphor, humans wandering in the desert of Reason discovered a garden containing all the fruits rejected by Reason. The forbidden garden of the rejected parts of the self--emotion, clusters of involuntary associated memory, illusions of madness and dreams, chaotic Unreason--had to be scaled if its insights were to be gained (or rather, descended to--this garden was subterranean, the basement of the soul). And who was daring enough to risk this descent into chaos for the fruit of knowledge?--the daimonic shaman in the form of the Romantic, and ultimately the psychiatrist.

Rousseau and the Romantic Voice

An early note of dissonance in the optimistic harmony of the Enlightenment was heard when Jean Jacques Rousseau (1712-1778) ended his friendship and philosophical ties with both Diderot and Hume. Like other Enlightenment thinkers he believed in the existence of natural laws but saw human interference with these laws as the source of evil. He stressed conscience rather than Reason, disagreed that civilization was a sign of progress in the human condition, suggested that the sciences have not benefitted humankind, and argued that we should look to children, savages, and nature for goodness and creativity.

His *Confessions*, modeled after St. Augustine's, were widely read and are still popular today. The book created a new, intensely personal style of autobiography and established the tone of Romantic sensibility: hiding nothing, revealing doubt and shame, expressing dissatisfaction with what Leibniz (echoing the medievalists) called the "best of all possible worlds." It also put the doubting, willful individual at the center of the stage (Sigismund of *Life's a Dream* shaking the bars of his cage and wailing for truth and justice), at the start of a lonely quest to go where no man has ever gone before, to the heights of heavenly inspiration or the daimonic pits of hell and madness, in search of understanding. This focus on the creative individual, a force unto himself, links Rousseau's *Confessions* with such diverse personal expressions as Donald Grant Mitchell's slobbery *Reveries of a Bachelor* (1850) and *Dream Life* (1851), Thomas de Quincy's disturbing *Confessions of an Opium Eater* (1822), and the surrealistic *Aurelia*, the spiritual autobiography of the mad and suicidal Gerard de Nerval (1808-1855).

Rousseau's was a gentle vision compared with the angry alienation of Baudelaire whose *Flowers of Evil* are not the sentimental daisies of the rural ruin but surrealistic, monstrous life-forms that grow, twisted and hideous, in the anomic, cruel cities created by the blight of "progress." The optimistic voice of the Enlightenment had not predicted tuberculosis and cholera, swollen bellies and cavernous faces, or the wholesale and indiscriminate slaughter of the French Revolution. Is it possible, Baudelaire asks, that the blind men tapping their way across the streets of Paris, their blind eyes gazing dreamily upward, can see an order, beauty, and meaning that he is unable to see, even in the fitful, lonely dreams of his imagination?

The path to Baudelaire was paved with wistful reveries, the sentimental vibrations of nerves/heart/Organ of Sensibility, mystical visions, prophetic revelations, creation of myth, transcendent communion with nature, seizure by the dark power of the Imagination, the use of opium to recreate the dream state, the glorification of poetry as "rationalized dreams." In all of these versions of Romanticism, the artist (like the modern version of the Scientist--for example, Sinclair Lewis's *Arrowsmith*) was a violently self-centered hero who espoused following an inner vision rather than rules. And in the development of the Romantic voice, the dream played multiple roles.

Romantic Uses of the Dream

A forerunner of Baudelaire, and translated into French by him, Edgar Allan Poe (1809-1849) used dreams to represent the boundary between life and death, sanity and insanity, and the enormous gulf between the hideous, confining limitations of real life and the ecstasies of an ideal but unreal paradise. Sleep, death, and insanity are regions of mystery, and dreams lie at their boundaries--a royal road to the unself--sometimes transcendently divine, and sometimes hideous. The shamanic hero wandering through the land of shadows sometimes finds jewels and secret cures for cancer, but is just as likely to be eaten by monsters.

The dream also served as a form by which the "real" world could be criticized. Percy Bysshe Shelley (1792-1822) argues that poets are "the institutors of laws and the founders of civil society" whose imaginative rather than reasoning powers can assess true value and thus serve as instruments of moral goodness. Imagination provides the "dreams of what ought to be, or may be" (see Clark 1966:279).

Dreams are used by Thomas Hood (1799-1845) in moralistic statements that would resemble *Pilgrim's Progress* if they were not so unique. In "Miss Kilmansegg and Her Precious Leg," a miserly woman with an artificial gold leg dreams that she is turned to gold--obviously a warning against her greedy obsession with wealth. Because she does not heed the moralistic warning in her dream, she is murdered by her husband, who brains her with the golden leg.

When the Romantics called attention to the negative consequences of "progress"--urbanization, child labor in the factories, the destruction of traditional communities--they often used the dream as a way of conveying their criticism and their hopes. Like the allegorical dream vision of the Middle Ages, the dream was a useful device for cultural innovation, for trying out new ideas. In the Romantic reaction, it was used to present dangerous, frightening, or unacceptable ideas, as if to say, "I didn't say this, my dream did"--a strategy similar to that adopted by Robert Louis Stevenson who, as a good Scottish Calvinist, knew that he should be good, so he invented Mr. Hyde, thus separating his bad impulses from his good ones for the explicit purpose of enjoying fully the process of being bad, without guilt.

In *Natural Supernaturalism* (1971), M. H. Abrams argues that many of the early Romantic poets interpreted the French Revolution as an apocalyptic event heralding the return of a lost Golden Age. When the political apocalypse failed, they turned to "apocalypse by imagination" (Abrams 1971:334)--a religious vision fully realized by William Blake in his *Four Zoas, Jerusalem*, and *Milton*.

Blake attributed to Los (the power of imagination, who eventually becomes synonymous with Jesus Christ, and ultimately with the essence of human identity) the ability to redeem humankind from the tyranny of oppressive laws imposed by Urizen, the Reasoning Power. In the ultimate of Romantic hubris, Blake resurrects Milton, fuses with him, purifies him of his respect for Reason, and together they unite with Los to recreate the world in the image of the imaginative poet.

The Fall of Hyperion: A Dream (1819) by John Keats (1795-1821) is a Romantic allegorical dream vision that warns against the misuse of the imagination, instead of perpetuating its architecture. Keats is a Romantic Empiricist who feels uncomfortable with the self-indulgent escapism of many dream poems. His earlier "The Eve of St. Agnes" is an ironic seduction-by-dream. The rake, Porphyro, pretends to be the "vision of delight" that young virgins hope to see on St. Agnes's Eve and steals into Madeline's chamber, wafting scented sweets and singing sweet music to her sleeping senses. When Madeline awakes, she mistakenly assumes that he is a vision and proclaims her love for him, whereupon "Into her dream he melted, as the rose/Blendeth its odour with the violet,--/Solution sweet," only to call her from sleep when St. Agnes's moon sets--"No dream, alas!" Although tempted by impossible dreams, Keats prefers those rooted in reality--"Beauty is truth, truth beauty--that is all/Ye know on earth, and all ye need to know"; and when the subjects of his poems awake, the distinction between waking to illusion and waking to reality is often painfully clear.

The poet-dreamer of *The Fall of Hyperion* begins his journey in a pastoral setting representing long-lost innocence, where he eats the "refuse" of a meal left behind by "angel" or "our Mother Eve." The drink he has during the meal puts him to sleep, and he "wakes" to the reality of Paradise lost, old myths destroyed. The incense that burns on the altar threatens to put him to sleep again; the sleep of innocence has become deadly, stifling, and paralytic. His Virgil, Moneta, encourages him not to escape from the world but to endure its pain, and to seek "no wonder but the human face." He must learn not to be a "dreamer," creating self-indulgent, unattainable illusions, but a true poet, someone who offers balm, a "sage;/A Humanist, physician to all men." But when Moneta gives him the imaginative power to see "as a god sees," Keats's vision, as a creative poet, falters, and he is left, like the ancient gods, paralyzed with "the load of this eternal quietude." The Romantic vision is potentially as sterile as the Rationalist vision. Keats probably would have recognized, with joy, the poetic resolution of truth and beauty in the transcendent realism of William Carlos Williams's "The Emperor of Ice Cream," Wallace Stevens's "The Blue Guitar," and the insightful science that produced models of evolution, DNA, and a universe composed of strings--as organic and harmonious, as true and beautiful, as any Grecian urn.

STALKING THE EMPIRICAL MIND

Descartes's separation of mind and body reflected the age-old dualism in Western culture of corporeal and intellectual, phenomenal and noumenal. What made it unusual was that it occurred in a context in which rational, empirical investigation of the phenomenal world was considered important. The resulting psychology was paradoxical: a detached mind deducting the logic of itself, independent of the evidence of the body. Simple, clear ideas constituted the building blocks of knowledge, and all other mental phenomena--emotions, distorted memories, illusions, and dreams--belonged to the trivial realms of bodily experience.

The associationists: John Locke, David Hume, and David Hartley and their successors, the Scottish School of Philosophy: Thomas Reid, Dugald Stewart, and Thomas Brown, asserted that the mind could also know reality through the senses; but they differ little from Descartes in their emphasis on conscious thought. Sensory experience was recorded in memory and linked through patterns of association, and "meaning" resulted from the combination of two or more sensory elements.

Toward the latter half of the eighteenth century, French writers became interested in mental states other than rational waking consciousness. For example, Diderot's *Encyclopedie* states:

In the strictest sense, we are dreaming all the time, that is to say that as soon as sleep has taken possession of our mental operations, the mind is subject to an uninterrupted series of representations and perceptions; but sometimes they are so confused or so dimly registered, that they do not leave the slightest trace, and this is in fact what we call "deep sleep;" but we would be wrong to regard it as a total absence of any sort of perception, as complete mental inertia. (Almansi and Beguin 1986: 42)

The perceptions of non-rational states, *etats seconds*, were used in dream narratives by Charles Nodier, Honore de Balzac, Alexander Dumas, Victor Hugo, and Gerard de Nerval, and twentieth-century writers have detected the presence of ideas that resemble a personal and collective unconscious long before Freud and Jung (see Knapp 1977, Porter 1979).

In a book that reflects the humanistic, empirical, and utopian melange of the French Revolution ("It was the best of times, it was the worst of times," as Dickens would later say), Pierre Cabanis's *Rapports du physique et du moral de l'homme* (1799) concluded that the twitches that occur in guillotined bodies were reflex actions and did not signify conscious awareness of pain on the part of the beheaded person. Cabanis developed a physiological hierarchy that presages Sir Charles Sherrington's progressive integration of the nervous system: At the lowest level, in the spinal cord, unconscious reflex action occurs in response to stimuli; at a higher level, semiconscious, semi-integrated activities occur; conscious volition, occurring in the brain, belongs to the highest level. He made a direct correlation between mental complexity and complexity of the nervous system. In *The Factors of Insanities* (1894), Hughlings Jackson linked this model with Darwin's evolutionary model to suggest that levels most recently acquired in evolution were most easily deranged.

Today brain and mind are considered equivalent, but in the psychology of the eighteenth and nineteenth centuries, the progress in physical studies did not always translate into the language of mind, which continued to wrestle with the philosophical issue of the soul. In a conception of mind accepted by the Scottish School, ultimately rejected by the hard-core associationists, and more fully developed by the Germans (for example, Christian Wolff's *Rational Psychology* [1734], Kant's *Critique of Pure Reason* [1781], and later Gestalt psychology), the mind was more than a peddlar's pack filled with associated clumps of memory; it was a unified expression of the faculties of the soul. Mind was, in effect, the soul carrying out its functions; thus the process of remembering was possible because of the soul's faculty of, or capacity for, or power of, memory. These prime causes or capacities which could only be accepted, not explained, operated on sensory experience. In *Elements of the Philosophy of the Human Mind* (1791), Dugald Stewart divided the powers of the mind (soul) into consciousness, external perception, attention, conception, abstraction, memory, judgment and reason, association of ideas, and imagination (dreaming is discussed not under "imagination," but as a subsection of the association of ideas). In addition to Hume's principles of resemblance, contiguity, and cause and effect, Stewart postulates principles such as contrast, habit, and the relationship of premise to conclusion.

According to Stewart, dreams are the mechanical products of association. Dream thoughts succeed one another according to the law of association, as these laws are modified by the dreamer's bodily associations and his thoughts and words before falling asleep--mathematicians dream of math problems, and so on. Dreams are more intense than waking experience because the faculties of will or judgment are suspended.

Imagination is a dangerous power, an entity independent of the intellect, that can counteract the "normal" process by which sense perceptions impress the mind. Madness results when the mind is taken over by the imagination and is cut off from external reality. On the other hand, imagination is the wellspring of new ideas and human improvement.

For a while, the mind had so many faculties that it resembled the assemblage of parts described earlier of the Homeric Greeks. They popped out all over, so that a new "science"--phrenology ("the study of the mind"--Greek *phren*)--was invented. A high forehead signified possession of the "organ of veneration"; people had bumps of acquisitiveness and bumps of hope, bumps of destructiveness and bumps of caution, bumps of mirthfulness, and even bumps of bibation (noted by authors concerned with temperance). Run by the engineer of intellect and haunted by the imagination, the nineteenth-century mind was an ungainly machine.

In the context of the Romantic Movement, mind soon began to resemble a Gothic mansion with secret rooms, hidden chambers, and a basement (see Bachelard 1969). As the imagination gained in power and became a creative force rather than shadowy interference with "real" thoughts (run by Reason), the unconscious came into being, and the basement opened out onto a vast landscape.

Nathaniel Hawthorne created powerful images of such landscapes. In "The Hall of Fantasy," he portrays imagination in architectural terms, reminiscent of Jung's use of the house as a way of analyzing the human soul. The spacious main hall has a lofty dome with windows that let in "the light of heaven" through stained, pictured glass; but beneath this level are "gloomy cells, which communicate with the infernal regions, and where monsters and chimeras are kept in confinement, and fed with all unwholesomeness" (quoted in Gollin 1979:41). This architectural structure "is separated from ordinary life, yet accessible to everyone" and may be entered "by the universal passport of a dream" or through poetic inspiration, prophetic visions, or madness.

Hawthorne frequently equated heart and mind or saw the mind as the intellectual counterpart of the heart, which was the vessel of passion, morality, and conscience; and in one creative image, he said that the Human Heart was "to be allegorized as a cavern; at the entrance there is sunshine, and flowers growing about it. You step within, but a short distance, and begin to find yourself surrounded with a terrible gloom, and monsters of divers kinds; it seems like Hell itself" (Gollin 1979:380). At the same time, as Hawthorne makes clear in "The Hall of Fantasy," this region enables him to "spiritualize the grossness of this actual life and to prefigure a state of eternity" (Gollin 1979:41). He reaches this land through the spirit, "the active element of consciousness that transcends the limits of waking life and the limits of mortality" (Gollin 1979:42). A dreamer must be strong to resist madness; only a person of strong will may traverse this land of awful wonders.

This dream landscape of the heart/soul/mind, a melange of scientific and Romantic influences, was populated by *doppelgangers*, animal spirits, pagan gods, Milton's Satan and Faust's Mephistopheles, Jung's *anima*, non-Western primitives, the abnormal, immoral or amoral, mad, timeless, changeless, hidden, sexually unrepressed--everything that Reason and the day world was not. Creative people were believed to have special access to this world via inspiration, madness, or some special sensitivity. All children, non-Western primitives, and women were believed to be closer to this world--children and savages by virtue of their being less constrained by Reason, women by virtue of an extra set of nerves that increased their sensibility and interfered with their Reason (Brown 1959:184)--but everyone entered it during their dreams.

A person's physiognomy (from the Greek for "the art of judging persons by their features") was the physical manifestation of moral strengths and weaknesses. The eye, especially when it teared, spoke the language of the soul, or rather, the language of the faculty of Sensibility (which resided in the sensorium, sometimes identified as the heart, and sometimes as the soul). It was vitally necessary to allow the faculty of Sensibility to express itself, especially in tears. To prevent tears caused bloody noses, bleeding hearts, delirium, and convulsions (Brown 1959:79). Some people possessed a mysterious power of sympathy called "animal magnetism," or mesmerism, that to many constituted scientific proof of the existence of the soul. With this power of attraction, people moved minds, won sympathy, captured hearts, and in the novel *Henry Russell*, abolished slavery, outlawed war, cured intemperance, and ushered in the millennium (Brown 1959:186).

The Locus of Mental Illness

The separation of mind and body, and an Enlightenment commitment to the body as a basis of explaining the mind, created confusing categories of human behavior, including "mental illness." What we now call mental illness was once explained as possession by evil spirits, requiring methods of exorcism. During the Renaissance, medieval possession became naturalistic illness (see Sarbin 1969 for a discussion of Teresa of Avila's role in saving her nuns from the Inquisition; also see the role that Pinel played during the late-eighteenth century in French mental asylums). With secularization of the divine, and with the Enlightenment-Romantic construction of the Freudian personality, the demonic was confined to the basement of our rejected self, to which we must go to perform our own exorcism (assisted by the daimonic shaman--the psychiatrist--who specializes in such journeys).

The desire to find a physical locus of behavior produced many cultural formulations, such as speculations about physiognomy, phrenology, and mesmerism, and as with all good scientific theories of the time, a functioning machine required a source of energy (Freud's id replaced Will and other faculties of the soul as the prime cause). Many physicians in the eighteenth and nineteenth centuries claimed that all forms of mental illness could be reduced to physical causes--inheritance, brain lesions, syphilis, alcoholism, and so on. The distinction between "organic" and "functional" disorders resulted from a blending of these different psychological explanations (physical and philosophical), and in particular from attempts to explain mesmerism.

Entirely different from the physical-philosophical explanations of "mental illness" are social and cultural explanations that have developed from the sociocultural epistemology of William Robertson Smith and Emile Durkheim. Intellectual heirs of Locke's *tabula rasa*, Robertson Smith and Durkheim explored the idea that our categories of knowing derive from the society in which we live. Only then did psychology begin to accept that "internal" disorders might be a product of sane behavior in an insane social environment (see the numerous and insightful writings of Thomas Szasz, in particular *The Myth of Mental Illness*).

Franz Mesmer (1734-1815) studied medicine in Vienna. His graduation thesis, *De planetarum Influxu* (1766), was a development of the astrological ideas of the sixteenth-century physician, Paracelsus, who said that a person's health could be influenced by the stars, which exerted a magnetic effect. A few years later Mesmer witnessed a set of cures that used magnetic plates; and in the same year that America was declaring her independence, he became convinced, through the demonstrations of a priest named Gassner, that the human hand was also capable of magnetizing ("animal magnetism"). In Paris, at that time the intellectual center of the world, he developed a salon to cure patients by increasing or decreasing the flow of magnetic fluid.

In a scheme reminiscent of pseudo-psychological self-help organizations today, he offered group treatments in which patients gathered around a trough filled with magnetized iron filings, mirrors, and iron rods (Mesmer's *baquet*), received the magnetic influence from the filings, and had "fits" or "crises," after which they were supposed to get well. His successes were astounding. The established medical community (in the form of the French Academy of Sciences) appointed a committee to investigate his claims. The committee, including Benjamin Franklin, ambassador from the recently established United States of America, concluded that animal magnetism did not exist. However, they did not explain why so many people who believed themselves to be magnetized were cured, and mesmerism spread to Germany, England, and the United States, where it joined forces with other fads such as phrenology (see the journal *Preno-magnet*, which documented what happened when magnetic hands were placed over certain regions of the skull, thus stimulating the faculty that was located underneath). Mesmerism was rescued from the grabbag of charlatanism by an English surgeon, James Braid, who recognized the psychological nature of the phenomenon, changed the name mesmerism to neurypnology and then coined the terms hypnotism and hypnosis--terms accepted by the medical profession by the middle of the nineteenth century. Mesmerism, alias hypnotism, was the first "paradoxical sleep" (the term given by twentieth-century neurophysiologists to dreaming sleep).

Hypnotism could be used to treat mental "illness" that was not apparently organic in origin. Functional disorders were themselves divided into neuroses and psychoses. Neuroses were disorders of the emotions or of the intellect and were considered exaggerated expressions of normal processes. Psychoses, on the other hand, were extreme disorders, characterized by the withdrawal of persons from "real" life, into a world of the imagination.

Freud and the Secret Wishes of the Soul

Sigmund Freud (1856-1939) received his M.D. from the University of Vienna in 1881 and returned there as *professor extraordinarius* in 1902. The University of Vienna prided itself on its empirical, scientific, materialist orientation, and stressed energy and evolution rather than vital spirits and the soul. Freud's early experiments centered on the testes of the eel and on the development of medullar pathways in fetal brains. In later years he was horrified by Jung's mysticism and prided himself on his scientific objectivity.

Shortly after receiving his M.D., Freud studied for several months in Paris with Jean Martin Charcot, from whom he learned hypnosis, and when he began practicing neurology, he used hypnosis to treat "functional" (non-organic) disorders. He learned from a colleague, Josef Breuer, that hysterical symptoms could be overcome if the patient were allowed to talk about the conditions under which these symptoms first occurred, and thereafter abandoned hypnosis and began to develop the "cathartic method" (*Studies in Hysteria* 1893-1895). Eventually he withdrew from neurology and developed his method (free association, transference, analysis of dreams) to which he gave the name psychoanalysis. After *The Interpretation of Dreams* was published in 1900, psychoanalysis spread through Viennese medical circles and international meetings, was used to treat war neuroses during World War I, and quickly invaded American psychiatry. In 1921, J. Arthur Thomson, in *The Outline of Science*, referred to psychoanalysis as the modern psychology.

Although initially interested in treating "abnormal" patients, Freud expanded his theory of psychoanalysis to explain puzzling events in "normal" behavior (dreams, slips of the tongue, jokes), the structure of the personality (id, ego, and superego), the development of different personality types (as the result of resolving conflicts posed by different stages of psychosexual development), problems of modern society, and even myths and the origin of human culture. The basic assumptions for psychoanalysis were established in *The Interpretation of Dreams*, a book that has echoed through the twentieth century not because it was a scientific masterpiece but because it synthesized, and thus validated, important cultural themes.

The central symbol in this synthesis is the dream. The dream expresses the secret wishes of the soul (in particular, Eros, although Freud later added Thanatos--the death instinct). The dream is the arena in which the forces for selfish, destructive evil struggle with the forces of ethics and the reality principle. It is a partially censored message, like an allegory or an oracle, that must be deciphered, with all the skills of a good allegorical hermeneutician, and it is a bridge by which Freud, psychiatrists, and all initiates in the mystic order are able to travel to the forbidden regions of mind and culture. (For an innovative science fiction version of this journey, see Roger Zelazny's *The Dream Master*.)

Like a good scientific theory, psychoanalysis comes packaged with its own energy source, the pseudo-biological instincts of the "id" (Spinoza's Will, Hobbes's Pleasure). It explains development of the organism (through psychosexual stages) and of the species as well (its origin in *Totem and Taboo*, and its apocalypse in *Civilization and its Discontents*). However much he was a Rousseauan Romantic, Freud also remained the constrained Victorian, a voyeur gazing at the forbidden paradise of the internal garden, only making trips when doing his scientific duty. Jung, however, set up camp there.

Jung: Freud's Doppelganger

In his autobiography, Jung defines the "shadow" as the "inferior part of the personality," the sum of all:

personal and collective psychic elements which, because of their incompatibility with the chosen conscious attitude, are denied expression in life and therefore coalesce into a relatively autonomous "splinter personality" with contrary tendencies in the unconscious. The shadow behaves compensatorily to consciousness. (1963:386-87)

The shadow, or *anima*, or *doppelganger* (double-walker) reaches "back into the realm of our animal ancestors," comprises morally reprehensible characteristics but is also the source of creativity and is, above all, the source to which we must go to be whole.

Jung saw himself as the necessary shadow to Freud's scientific viewpoint and as a more complete person than Freud--someone who had succeeded in embracing his *doppelganger*, in linking art with science. As a student he was interested in spiritualism, read Kant's *Dreams of a Spirit Seer* followed by seven volumes of Swedenborg, and wrote "On the Psychology and Pathology of So-Called Occult Phenomena" (1902) as his doctoral dissertation. His concept of synchronicity (the idea that all things are in sympathy and thus connected in time and space) was, he believed, objective reality rather than occult mysticism.

Jung clearly recognized that Freud's writings about the unconscious reflected deeply rooted cultural patterns rather than "objective" scientific fact.

Just as the psychically stronger agency is given "divine" or "daimonic" attributes, so the "sexual libido" took over the role of a *deus absconditus*, a hidden or concealed god . . . . The advantage of the transformation for Freud was, apparently, that he was able to regard the numinous principle as scientifically irreproachable and free from all religious taint. (Jung 1963:151)

Freud, said Jung, was "a man in the grip of his daimon" (Jung 1963:153) because he did not realize the spiritual significance of sexuality.

However, Jung was in the grip of the same daimon. He wanted, like modern-day Creationists, to turn religion into science. "Sexuality is of the greatest importance as the expression of the chthonic spirit. That spirit is the other face of God, the dark side of the God-image. The question of the chthonic spirit has occupied me ever since I began to delve into the world of alchemy" (Jung 1963:168).

Alchemy, like psychoanalysis, uses the scientific framework to justify mystical belief. Alchemy is a historical counterpart of the psychology of the unconscious.

Jung saw himself allied with Nietzsche, with whose myth of the Superman he was fascinated and about whom he wrote (bringing more charges of mysticism from empirically minded colleagues). Jung saw himself, like Nietzsche, creating a new heroic morality that would represent the highest passion and creativity--thus transcending conventions of good and evil, science and mysticism. Although he says he rejected the myth of the superman (see Jung 1963:171-181), he saw himself as playing a higher role, the ultimate superman--the Messiah. He believed that God had sent him the dreams, and "From the beginning I had a sense of destiny" (1963:48). He conversed with his spirit-guide, Phelemon, and was haunted by an ancestral archetype, the Gnostic Basilides, who forced him to write "The Seven Sermons of the Dead written by Basilides in Alexandria, the City where the East toucheth the West"--"Like a medium, it gives the dead a chance to manifest themselves" (1963:190-191).

Jung saw himself, as did the Romantics before him, as counterweights to Western culture's Rationalism. The dream was a lifeline to the primeval, collective past, the primitive as opposed to the rational Western ego. He visited Africa in search of "a psychic observation post outside the sphere of the European" (1963:244). In Tunisia he described Arabs as primitive (their egos had no autonomy), Europeans as more advanced (they had will and were able to direct their attention). In a dream he wrestled with an Arab prince, pushed his head under water, and then forced him to read (1963:242). When he interpreted the dream, he saw the Arab as an ethnic shadow, or what he perceived to be the naive, unsophisticated, unconscious, vital self, in contrast with the European who was the equivalent of the ego--rational and less vital. He conceived of Africans as prehistoric Europeans, or Europeans asleep and dreaming. When he dreamed that his American Negro barber in Tennessee was trying to give him kinky Negro hair, he awoke with terror and wrote that he was afraid of "going black" (1963:245, 272). To him the dream was a warning from his unconscious, a signal of spiritual peril, and he cut his African tour short.

Throughout his memoirs, Jung tells his dreams, using them to legitimize his insights, as if they were divine messages, with an aura of authority. The dreams not only gave him insight but they demanded his attention, like gods, threatening madness or even death: "If you don't follow through on these thoughts, you must shoot yourself" (1963:180). Although he knew that his ideas would result in his being branded a mystic, his dreams pointed out to him his "destiny."

Jung describes himself as being driven by a "fateful compulsion," and acting as "a compensation for our times," "the counterweight to the conscious world"

(Jung 1963:222). He belongs, in this sense, to the Romantics. Jung's hubris is to impose his messianic complex on the world and call it science.

8

Post-Freud Postscript

R. A. Underwood (1970) begins his article, "Myth, Dream, and the Vocation of Contemporary Philosophy," with a dream. He is in a Swiss village near the central fountain. The village is deserted, and gradually the fountain stops flowing, and a flame emerges. Suddenly the village fills with people running and shouting--but no sounds come out, only letters of the alphabet pouring out like vomit until the sky is filled and the people drowning in a sea of words.

A. O. Watts (1970), in "Western Mythology: Its Dissolution and Transformation," says that the quest for knowledge in the West is to ascertain the laws, the Word, established at the beginning and controlling all processes going on today. If we can understand the word of God, we can understand the past, present, and future. This religious quest is the foundation of Western science: to make matter subservient to will and achieve immortality.

In the Judeo-Christian tradition, the human world is conceived of as intricately connected to the divine. The human world is the arena in which God brings into being the lineal progression toward an apocalyptic vision--the struggle between good and evil, the return of the Messiah, Christ as the incarnation of the divine, the overthrow of demons, the emergence of the Word in history. Over the past two thousand years this structure has remained, although the divine has become secularized.

Freud "discovered" the mind in the context of Renaissance individualism, Cartesian rationalism, Romantic resurrection of the unconscious from the graveyard of Reason, passionate commitment to the empirical investigation of the phenomenal world, and above all, in the dualistic context of the Judeo-Christian tradition. Anthropology continues this tradition, this hermeneutic quest, interpreting the messages of the divine in language and culture.

Paul Ricoeur asks in *Freud and Philosophy* (1970), "How do desires achieve speech?" From biblical exegesis to philosophy, anthropology to psychoanalysis, he is looking for a "comprehensive philosophy of language to account for the multiple functions of the human act of signifying." All human action is the disguised expression of desire. When confronted with a text to interpret, one no longer moves up the Augustinian hierarchy to higher truths, but down into the basement of desire--Michel Foucault's "archaeology of knowledge."

The "deeper" we go, the more sacred the ground. In the quest for the dreamer's history that is unfolded through psychoanalysis or by tracing the roots of the dream back to its source, the psychiatrist and the dreamer are returning to original creation (personal or archetypal) in order to achieve future transformations, future creations. The anthropologist who is also hermeneutician, literary critic, and deconstructionist seeks to reveal the unknowable name of god and thus become God. If we know the nine million names of God--all the allegorical representations of Love in *The Romance of the Rose*--we become God, and the universe ceases to exist; history is no longer necessary.

Hermeneutics is a theory of rules that presides over an interpretation of a text. A dream is like an allegory; it is a double-meaning linguistic expression that requires interpretation. Some texts are relatively easy to interpret because they use common symbols (for example, myth and ritual); others are personal and idiosyncratic. As we go from the allegorical dream vision of the Middle Ages that everyone understood to the Freudian dream that only the dreamer with the help of the psychiatrist comes to understand, the unified mirror of culture (the didactic, educational formula perpetuated by the authoritative structure of the medieval world) becomes a splintered mirror; and like a group of Narcissuses, we all gaze into our separate, splintered fragments. Occasionally we dream common dreams; or perhaps this is the imposition of a Freudian myth or a by-product of the way our brain files information (see Jonathan Winson, *Brain and Psyche*). This image of separate, isolated dreamers, each looking into their own mirrors and imposing their own interpretations on their images, is the lonely, fragmented vision of Deconstructionism. Perhaps one of the reasons Freud was so popular was that he created a new myth, a new mirror into which we can all gaze and find a common meaning. (Hush, hush, don't challenge Scholastic wisdom--of course the stick is a symbol of a penis.)

Perhaps, post-Freud, unable to make sense of the symbols of others, we adopt a post-modern theory of symbols that says it is impossible to understand anyone else; the world we create is our own, continuously unfolding. We even lack our own history. Our creations become history, and we strive for fame because we strive to become the god of our history, remembered by others, because we cannot remember ourselves. Americans in particular are continuously redefining themselves, inventing new identities.

Thus post-modernism is like Romanticism--a reaction against the orderly promise of Reason--which itself will promote a new communal understanding of the underworld. In the name of shamanic individualism and creativity, we destroy worlds. We wallow in the divine garbage of our idiosyncratic souls as we pursue our shamanic quests, but presume to be *the* Messiah who writes the history of others.

In this post-post-modern world, we alternate between the ruses of creativity and the desire for unification with the One, with a system of analyzing symbols that seems to promise on the one hand personal control over the world, and on the other communion with an elite set of occult priests.

In Western culture, what began as an attempt to understand the manifestation of the divine in the human world has become a glorification of the self. The hermeneutics of psychoanalysis, linguistics, and structuralist anthropology is the ultimate conceit of Renaissance humanism and its secularization of the divine in the context of the Judeo-Christian tradition.

There is an ultimate question that stems from the possibilities, errors, and follies of the Renaissance, Enlightenment, and Romantic Movement: Is it possible for humans to be realistic? We "know" through our cultural systems and can also reflect on and compare these cultural ways of knowing, thereby generating contrasts and comparisons--new places to stand by which to grasp, like blind men holding on to different parts of an elephant, pieces of the dark fabric of the universe. The still, small voice of empirical realism sometimes goes counter to cultural systems, although it can also become a central tenet of culture.

Science-humanism is a voice of realism that has been heard, sometimes loudly, in Western history, but it is frequently drowned by other patterns in the Judeo-Christian tradition. The materialism of biology and economics are often placed on the side of the Devil--Communism, Marxism, "secular humanism"; but it does not have to be placed there symbolically. Biological and economic perspectives help us understand why we exist or disappear, why species survive or perish, how complex economies avoid, sink, or rise above the factors that cause depression. Science does not, as method, destroy "spirit" or "will"; it is morally neutral. We can weave science into the interpretive fabric of our meaning system in ways that perpetuate and ennoble what it means to be human. In his awareness of the historical-cultural context in which science emerges and is used, Stephen Jay Gould is one of the strongest voices of our era for the majesty of complex realism.

I take heart from Mary Reilly's book, *Dr. Jekyll's Housekeeper*: The symbol of Dr. Jekyll and Mr. Hyde is no longer interpreted as a parable of our dual natures, intended to encourage a moral journey toward mastering our evil instincts; rather, it is a warning that dualistic extremism is itself the problem. The either-or dialectic of Western culture will continue to swing us between the extremes of the Middle Ages and the Enlightenment unless we learn to recognize the symptoms of our cultural system.

THE MUSHROOM AND THE MYSTIC ROSE

"The heart--have you found the heart?" In Jean Genet's *Miracle of the Rose*, a homosexual love story set in the death wing of a prison, the executioners invade the prisoner's body, intricate corridors lined with mirrors, and enter the portal of the heart. The heart of the heart is an enormous red rose: "The Mystic Rose, murmured the chaplain." The executioners rape the heart, "pushing back the petals and crumpling them with their drunken hands, as a lecher who has been deprived of sex pushes back a whore's skirt." They reach the heart of the rose, which is a dark well, and, losing their balance, fall into its "deep gaze" (Almansi and Beguin 1986:94-97).

The deep well of Genet's modern allegory lies at the heart of the heart of the heart--the mysterious mycelium from which rose-mushrooms grow. Freud, in his vast synthesis, realized that he did not know it all. As grand a vista as he had sketched, as much as he had drawn upon the patterns of knowledge and meaning available to him in his cultural context, the dark beyond the boundary of knowing contained seeds of future patterns, new mushrooms to perceive, analyze, and appreciate.

To me, raised in a household of Freud, Enlightenment principles, and poetry, this is one of the most affecting passages in *The Interpretation of Dreams*. I grew up distrusting Freud because his ideas were used to control others, not to enhance understanding;   Leon Edel's *Stuff of Sleep and Dreams: Experiments in Literary Psychology* (1982) psychoanalyzes writers and reduces them to infants: "You're the way you are because of your mother/father." Hence, Thoreau becomes the spoiled son of a mousy father and a mother with grand airs, disliked by his neighbors. Kafka's *Castle* can be traced to a childhood experience of being shut out on a balcony by his father because he wanted a drink of water. I was frustrated, as a person committed to clear thinking and scientific testability, at what appeared to me to be an imposition of cultural interpretation on objective description. His observations were fascinating, but I bristled at his Victorian sexism and morality, and disdained his petty territorial battles.

Chucking Freud, I began, like any good *tabula rasa*, at the beginning, building up sensory impressions from the rudimentary experiments on sleep and dreams. But as Hume demonstrated, you can go only so far with mechanical associations guarded by skepticism and must begin to look for relationships, patterns, insights--an inductive-deductive process. And the most important step in getting a handle on dreams was to realize that they are not simply electrochemical explosions in an evolutionary context, but electrochemical explosions interpreted in a cultural context.

The major revolution in the history of thought that begins with the late nineteenth and twentieth century is the emergence of Robertson Smith/Durkheimian sociology. Categories of understanding no longer depend on sensory impressions or on a priori truths, but on the categories given to us by our culture. Thought and meaning are rooted in politico-economic conditions, but this does not reduce them to materialist by-products; they must be understand as themselves, and as part of a complex whole.

This book represents an approach that is, I believe, useful for all areas of understanding: Observe as carefully as you can the phenomenon in which you are interested; and then observe, to the extent that this is possible, the cultural categories within which you make your observations. Whatever synthesis you make, it will probably be an improvement over syntheses that do not take cultural categories into account, but it will always be limited. Beyond the boundaries of what we know, the mycelium awaits.

Bibliography

Abrams, M. H. *The Mirror and the Lamp: Romantic Theory and the Critical Tradition*. New York: W. W. Norton, 1958.

-------. *Natural Supernaturalism: Tradition and Revolution in Romantic Literature*. New York: W.W. Norton, 1971.

Almansi, Guido, and Claude Beguin. *Theatre of Sleep: An Anthology of Literary Dreams*. London: Pan Books, 1986.

Azouvi, Francois. "Woman as a Model of Pathology in the Eighteenth Century," *Diogenes* 115 (Fall 1981): 22-36.

Bachelard, Gaston. *Poetics of Space*. Translated by Maria Joks. Boston: Beacon Press, 1969.

Barfield, Owen. "Dream, Myth, and Philosophical Double Vision." In *Myths, Dreams, and Religion*, edited by Joseph Campbell. New York: E. P. Dutton, 1970, pp. 211-24.

Basso, Ellen B. "The Implications of a Progressive Theory of Dreaming." In *Dreaming: Anthropological and Psychological Interpretations*, edited by Barbara Tedlock. New York: Cambridge University Press, 1987.

Benziger, James. *Images of Eternity*. Carbondale: Southern Illinois University Press, 1962.

Birch, Frank, and J. B. Trend, eds. and tr. *Pedro Calderon de la Barca Life's a Dream*. Cambridge: W. Heffer and Sons, 1925.

Boorstin, D. J. "The Lost Arts of Memory," *The Wilson Quarterly* VIII, No. 2 (Spring 1984): 104-13.

Bowra, C. M. *The Greek Experience*. New York: New American Library, 1957.

-------. *The Romantic Imagination*. Cambridge: Harvard University Press, 1949.

Brown, Herbert Ross. *The Sentimental Novel in America, 1789-1860*. New York: Pageant Books, 1959 (1940).

Bullock-Kimball, Beatrice Susanne. *The European Heritage of Rose Symbolism and Rose Metaphors in View of Rilke's Epitaph Rose.* New York: Peter Lang, 1987.

Bunyan, John. *The Pilgrim's Progress: In the Similitude of a Dream.* New York: Collier Press, 1909.

Bush, Clive. *The Dream of Reason: American Consciousness and Cultural Achievement from Independence to the Civil War.* New York: St. Martin's Press, 1977.

Butcher, S. H., and A. Lang, tr. *The Odyssey of Homer.* New York: Collier and Sons, 1909.

Campbell, Joseph, ed. *Myths, Dreams, and Religion.* New York: E. P. Dutton, 1970.

Clark, David Lee, ed. *Shelley's Prose or The Trumpet of a Prophecy.* Albuquerque: University of New Mexico Press, 1966.

Clifford, James, and George E. Marcus, eds. *Writing Culture: The Poetics and Politics of Ethnography.* Los Angeles: University of California Press, 1986.

Coburn, Kathleen, ed. *The Notebooks of Samuel Taylor Coleridge.* New York: Bollingen Foundation, 1961.

Colville, Derek. Victorian Poetry and the Romantic Religion. Albany, New York: SUNY Press, 1970.

Crawford, W. S. *Synesius the Hellene.* London: Rivingtons, 1901.

Curtius, Ernst Robert. *European Literature and the Latin Middle Ages.* Translated by Willard R. Trask. New York: Pantheon Books, 1953.

Dahlberg, Charles, tr. *The Romance of the Rose.* Princeton: Princeton University Press, 1971.

Dawson, Christopher. *Religion and the Rise of Western Culture.* New York: Doubleday, 1958.

Desowitz, R. S. "How the Wise Men Brought Malaria to Africa: And Other Cautionary Tales of Human Dreams and Opportunistic Mosquitoes," *Natural History Magazine,* October 1976.

Dodds, E. R. *The Greeks and the Irrational.* Berkeley: University of California Press, 1951.

-------. *Pagan and Christian in an Age of Anxiety: Some Aspects of Religious Experience from Marcus Aurelius to Constantine.* Cambridge: Cambridge University Press, 1965.

Douglas, Mary. *Purity and Danger: An Analysis of the Concepts of Pollution and Taboo.* Boston: Ark Paperbacks, 1966.

------- and Aaron Wildavsky. *Risk and Culture: An Essay on the Selection of Technological and Environmental Dangers.* Los Angeles: University of California Press, 1982.

Dunlop, Charles E. M., ed. *Philosophical Essays on Dreaming.* Ithaca: Cornell University Press, 1977.

Dunn, Charles W., ed. *The Romance of the Rose.* New York: E. P. Dutton, 1962.

Eagleton, Terry. *Literary Theory: An Introduction.* Minneapolis: University of Minnesota Press, 1983.

Edel, Leon. *Stuff of Sleep and Dreams: Experiments in Literary Psychology.* New York: Harper and Row, 1982.

Edelstein, Emma J., and Ludwig Edelstein. *Asclepius: A Collection and Interpretation of the Testimonies.* 2 vols. Baltimore: Johns Hopkins University Press, 1945.

Eisner, Will. "Getting the Last Laugh: My Life in Comics," *New York Times Book Review,* 14 January, 1990.

Eliade, Mircea. *Cosmos and History: The Myth of the Eternal Return.* New York: Harper Torchbooks, 1959.

Ellis, F.S., ed. and tr. *The Romance of the Rose.* London: J. M. Dent, Aldine House, 1900.

Fabian, Johannes. "Dream and Charisma, 'Theories of Dreams' in the Jamaa-Movement (Congo)," *Anthropos* 61 (1966): 544-560.

Fallon, Ivan, and James Srodes. *Dream Maker: The Rise and Fall of John Z. de Lorean.* New York: G. P. Putnam's Sons, 1983.

Fernandez-Armesto, Felipe. *Before Columbus: Exploration and Colonization from the Mediterranean to the Atlantic, 1229-1492.* Philadelphia: University of Pennsylvania Press, 1987.

Finley, M. I. *The World of Odysseus.* Rev. ed. New York: Viking Press, 1978.

Fitz-Gerald, A. *The Essays and Hymns of Synesius of Cyrene.* 2 vols. Oxford: Oxford University Press, 1930.

Fleming, John V. *Reason and the Lover.* Princeton: Princeton University Press, 1984.

-------. *The Roman de la Rose: A Study in Allegory and Iconography.* Princeton: Princeton University Press, 1969.

Fliess, Robert. *The Revival of Interest in the Dream: A Critical Study of Post-Freudian Psychoanalytic Contributions.* New York: International Universities Press, Inc., 1953.

Foucault, Michel. *The Archaeology of Knowledge and the Discourse on Language.* New York: Harper Colophon Books, 1972.

Franz, Marie-Louise von. "The Dream of Descartes." In *Timeless Documents of the Soul,* edited by H. Jacobsohn, M. von Franz, and S. Hurwitz. Evanston: Northwestern University Press, 1968, pp. 57-147.

Freeman, Derek. "Human Nature and Culture." In *Man and the New Biology*, edited by R. O. Slatyer, et al. Camberra, Australia: Australia National University Press, 1970: 50-75.

Freud, Sigmund. *The Interpretation of Dreams*. Translated by James Strachey. London: Allen and Unwin, 1954.

Garber, M. B. *Dream in Shakespeare: From Metaphor to Metamorphosis*. New Haven: Yale University Press, 1974.

Garrod, H. W., ed. *John Keats, Poetical Works*. Oxford: Oxford University Press, 1970.

Gay, Peter. *The Enlightenment: An Interpretation*. New York: Vintage Books, 1968.

Glover, T. R. *The Conflict of Religions in the Early Roman Empire*. New York: Cooper Square Publishers, 1975 (1909).

Gollin, Rita K. *Nathaniel Hawthorne and the Truth of Dreams*. Baton Rouge: Louisiana State University Press, 1979.

Goodrich, Norma Lorre. *The Medieval Myths*. New York: Mentor Books, 1961.

Gouldner, Alvin W. *Enter Plato: Classical Greece and the Origins of Social Theory*. New York: Basic Books, 1965.

Gunn, Alan M.F. *The Mirror of Love: A Reinterpretation of "The Romance of the Rose."* Lubbock: Texas Tech Press, 1952.

Hamilton, Edith. *The Greek Way*. New York: W. W. Norton, 1964.

Hamilton, Mary. *Incubation, or the Cure of Disease in Pagan Temples and Christian Churches*. London: Marshall, Hamilton, Kent, 1906.

Harness, Charles L. *The Rose*. New York: Berkley Medallion Books, 1953.

Hawkes, Jacquetta. *History of Mankind: Cultural and Scientific Development*. New York: Mentor Books, 1965.

Heer, Friedrich. *The Medieval World*. New York: Mentor Books, 1961.

Hermann, Janet Sharp. *The Pursuit of a Dream*. Cambridge: Oxford University Press, 1981.

Herzfeld, Michael. *Anthropology Through the Looking-Glass: Critical Ethnography in the Margins of Europe*. Cambridge: Cambridge University Press, 1987.

Highbarger, Ernest Leslie. *The Gates of Dreams*. Oxford: Oxford University Press, 1940.

Hill, Brian. *Gates of Horn and Ivory: An Anthology of Dreams*. New York: Taplinger, 1967.

Hillman, J. *The Dream and the Underworld*. New York: Harper and Row, 1979.

Hobson, J. Allan, and Robert W. McCarley. "The Brain as a Dream State Generator: An Activation-Synthesis Hypothesis of the Dream Process," *American Journal of Psychiatry* 134, No. 12 (1977): 1335-48.

Hollister, C. Warren, ed. *Landmarks of the Western Heritage.* Vol. 1, *The Ancient Near East to 1789.* New York: John Wiley and Sons, 1973.

Huizinga, J. *The Waning of the Middle Ages: A Study of the Forms of Life, Thought and Art in France and the Netherlands in the XIVth and XVth Centuries.* New York: Doubleday, 1954.

Jaeger, Werner. *The Theology of the Early Greek Philosophers.* Oxford: Oxford University Press, 1947.

Jung, C. G. *Memories, Dreams, Reflections.* New York: Pantheon Books, 1963.

Kant, Immanuel. *Dreams of a Spirit-Seer: Illustrated by Dreams of Metaphysics.* New York: MacMillan, 1900.

Kitto, H. D. F. *The Greeks.* Baltimore: Penguin Books, 1957.

Kittredge, George Lyman. *Chaucer and his Poetry.* Cambridge: Harvard University Press, 1915.

Knapp, B. L. *Dream and Image.* Troy: Whitston, 1977.

Kroeber, A. L. *Configurations of Culture Growth.* Berkeley: University of California Press, 1944.

Le Goff, Jacques. *The Birth of Purgatory.* Translated by Arthur Goldhammer. Chicago: University of Chicago Press, 1984.

-------. *The Medieval Imagination.* Translated by Arthur Goldhammer. Chicago: The University of Chicago Press, 1988.

LeGuin, Ursula K. *The Language of the Night: Essays on Fantasy and Science Fiction.* Hastings-on-Hudson, NY: Ultramarine, 1979.

Longfellow, Henry Wadsworth, tr. *The Divine Comedy of Dante Alighieri.* Boston: James R. Osgood, 1871.

Lot, Ferdinand. *The End of the Ancient World: And the Beginnings of the Middle Ages.* New York: Harper and Row, 1961 (1913-1921).

Lovecraft, H. P. *The Dream-Quest of Unknown Kadath.* New York: Ballantine Books, 1970 (1939).

Lovejoy, Arthur. *The Great Chain of Being: A Study of the History of an Idea.* Cambridge: Harvard University Press, 1936.

Luria, Maxwell. *A Reader's Guide to the Roman de la Rose.* Hamden, Conn.: Archon Books, 1982.

Mannheim, Bruce. "A Semiotic of Andean Dreams." In *Dreaming: Anthropological and Psychological Interpretations*, edited by Barbara Tedlock. Cambridge: Cambridge University Press, 1987, pp. 132-53.

Manuel, Frank E. *The Eighteenth Century Confronts the Gods.* Cambridge: Harvard University Press, 1959.

Maritain, Jacques. *The Dream of Descartes.* Port Washington: Kennikat Press, 1969 (1944).

Martin, Terence. *The Instructed Vision.* Bloomington: Indiana University Press, 1961.

Mautner, F. H., and H. Hatfield, eds. *The Lichtenberg Reader: Selected Writings of G.. Lichtenberg*. Boston: Beacon Press, 1959.

McCallum, James Ramsay. *Abelard's Christian Theology*. Merrick, NY: Richwood, 1976.

McCarley, R. W., and J. A. Hobson. "The Forms of Dreams and the Biology of Sleep." In *Handbook of Dreams*, edited by B. B. Wolman. New York: van Nostrand Reinhold, 1979, pp. 76-130.

McGann, Jerome J. *The Romantic Ideology: A Critical Investigation*. Chicago: University of Chicago Press, 1983.

Messer, William Stuart. *The Dream in Homer and Greek Tragedy*. New York: Columbia University Press, 1918.

Miller, David L. "Orestes: Myth and Dream as Catharsis." In *Myths, Dreams, and Religion*, edited by Joseph Campbell. New York: E. P. Dutton, 1970, pp. 26-47.

Murray, Gilbert. *The Rise of the Greek Epic*. New York: Oxford University Press, 1960 (1907).

Niebuhr, Reinhold. *The Self and the Dramas of History*. New York: Scribner's, 1955.

Nisbet, Robert. *Social Change*. New York: Harper and Row, 1972.

O'Flaherty, W. D. *Siva: The Erotic Ascetic*. New York: Oxford University Press, 1973.

Osgood, C. G. *Boccaccio on Poetry*. New York: Liberal Arts Press, 1956.

Pandian, Jacob. *Anthropology and the Western Tradition: Toward an Authentic Anthropology*. Prospect Heights, Ill,: Waveland Press, 1985.

-------. *Culture, Religion, and the Sacred Self: A Critical Introduction to the Anthropological Study of Religion*. New York: Prentice-Hall, 1990.

Parman, Susan. "An Evolutionary Theory of Dreaming and Play." In *Forms of Play of Native North Americans*, edited by E. Norbeck and C. R. Farrer. St. Paul, Minn.: West Publishing, 1979, pp. 17-34.

-------. "*Orduighean*: A Dominant Ritual Symbol in the Free Church of the Scottish Highlands," *American Anthropologist* 92, No. 2, 1990.

-------. Organizer and Chair of Symposium, "Dream as a Cultural System: Mirror of Mind and Society." Southwestern Anthropological Association, San Diego, 26 March, 1983.

Patch, Howard Rollin. *The Other World According to Descriptions in Medieval Literature*. Cambridge: Harvard University Press, 1950.

Patterson, Frank Allen. *The Works of John Milton*. New York: Columbia University Press, 1931-1938.

Phillips, J. R. S. *The Medieval Expansion of Europe*. Oxford: Oxford University Press, 1988.

Pieper, Josef. *Scholasticism: Personalities and Problems of Medieval Philosophy*. Translated by Richard and Clara Winston. New York: McGraw-Hill, 1960.

Pirenne, Henri. *Medieval Cities: Their Origins and the Revival of Trade*. Princeton: Princeton University Press, 1952.

Porter, Laurence M. *The Literary Dream in French Romanticism: A Psychoanalytic Interpretation*. Detroit: Wayne State University Press, 1979.

Progoff, I. "Waking Dream and Living Myth." In *Myths, Dreams, and Religion*, edited by Joseph Campbell. New York: E. P. Dutton, 1970, pp. 176-95.

Raby, Frederic James Edward. *A History of Christian-Latin Poetry from the Beginnings to the Close of the Middle Ages*. 2d. ed. Oxford: Oxford Clarendon Press, 1953.

Ricoeur, Paul. *Freud and Philosophy: An Essay on Interpretation*. New Haven: Yale University Press, 1970.

Robinson, C. E. *Hellas*. Boston: Beacon Press, 1948.

Robinson, T. M. *Plato's Psychology*. Toronto: University of Toronto Press, 1970.

Rouse, W. H. D., tr. *Homer, The Iliad*. New York: New American Library, 1938.

Saberhagen, Fred. "Wings out of Shadow." In *Hallucination Orbit: Psychology in Science Fiction*, edited by I. Asimov, C.G. Waugh, and M.H. Greenberg. New York: Farrar, Straus, Giroux, 1983, pp. 173-95.

Sanday, Peggy. *Divine Hunger: Cannibalism as a Cultural System*. Cambridge: Cambridge University Press, 1986.

Sarbin, Theodore R. "The Scientific Status of the Mental Illness Metaphor." In *Changing Perspectives in Mental Illness* edited by Stanley C. Plog and Robert B. Edgerton. New York: Holt, Rinehart and Winston, 1969, pp. 9-31.

Schneider, H. *A History of American Philosophy*. New York: Columbia University Press, 1946.

Seward, Barbara. *The Symbolic Rose*. New York: Columbia University Press, 1960.

Silk, Mark. "Notes on the Judeo-Christian Tradition in America," *American Quarterly* 36, No. 1 (Spring 1984): 65-85.

Skeat, W. W. *A Concise Etymological Dictionary of the English Language*. New York: Perigee Books, 1980.

Snell, Bruno. *The Discovery of the Mind: The Greek Origins of European Thought*. New York: Harper Torchbooks, 1960.

Speroni, C. *The Aphorisms of Orazio Rinaldi, Robert Greene, and Lus Gracinn Dantisco*. Publications in Modern Philology, vol. 88. Los Angeles: University of California Press, 1968.

Stahl, William Harris, tr. *Ambrosius Aurelius Theodosius Macrobius: Commentary on the Dream of Scipio*. New York: Columbia University Press, 1952.

Steinberg, Leo. *The Sexuality of Christ in Renaissance Art and in Modern Oblivion*. New York: Pantheon Books, 1983.

Stewart, Dugald. *Elements of the Philosophy of the Human Mind*. Boston: Munroe, 1854 (1791).

Sullivan, Henry W. *Calderon in the German Lands and the Low Countries: His Reception and Influence, 1654-1980*. Cambridge: Cambridge University Press, 1983.

Taylor, Thomas, tr. *On the Mysteries of the Egyptians, Chaldeans and Assyrians*. 2d ed. London, 1895.

Underwood, R.A. "Myth, Dream, and the Vocation of Contemporary Philosophy." In *Myths, Dreams, and Religion*, edited by Joseph Campbell. New York: E. P. Dutton, 1970, pp. 225-53.

Vartanian, Aram. "Diderot and the Phenomenology of the Dream," *Diderot Studies* 8 (1966).

Veitch, John, ed. and tr. "Rene Descartes." In *The Rationalists*. Garden City, N. Y.: Dolphin Books, 1960.

Vossler, Karl. *Medieval Culture: An Introduction to Dante and His Times*. Vols. 1 and 2. New York: Frederick Ungar Publishing, 1966 (1929).

Wallace, Anthony F. C. *The Death and Rebirth of the Seneca*. New York: Vintage Books, 1969.

Watts, A. W. "Western Mythology: Its Dissolution and Transformation." In *Myths, Dreams, and Religion*, edited by Joseph Campbell. New York: E. P. Dutton, 1970, pp. 9-25.

Weitzman, Arthur J. "The Oriental Tale in the Eighteenth Century: A Reconsideration," *Studies in Voltaire and the Eighteenth Century* 58 (1967): 1839-55.

West, M.L., ed. *Theogony*. Oxford: Clarendon Press, 1966.

White, Robert J., tr. *The Interpretation of Dreams: Oneirocritica by Artemidorus*. Park Ridge, N. J.: Noyes Press, 1975.

Whyte, Lancelot. *The Unconscious Before Freud*. New York: St. Martin's Press, 1978.

Wieruszowski, Helene. *The Medieval University*. Princeton: D. Van Nostrand, 1966.

Wilder, A. N. "Myth and Dream in Christian Scripture." In *Myths, Dreams, and Religion*, edited by Joseph Campbell. New York: E. P. Dutton, 1970, pp. 68-90.

Wind, Edgar. *Pagan Mysteries in the Renaissance: An Exploration of Philosophical and Mystical Sources of Iconography in Renaissance Art.* New York: W. W. Norton, 1968.

Wolf, Eric R. *Europe and the People Without History.* Berkeley: University of California Press, 1982.

Wright, Thomas. *Anglo-Latin Satirical Poets and Epigrammatists of the Twelfth Century.* London: HMSO, 1872.

Yates, Frances. *The French Academies of the Sixteenth Century.* Nendeln, Liechtenstein: Kraus Reprint, 1968 (The Warburg Institute, University of London, 1947).

Yeats, W. B. *The Collected Poems of W. B. Yeats.* London: Macmillan, 1965.

Index

About the Author

Susan Parman has written several books and articles on a variety of subjects
that include the history of ideas, the evolution of the brain, the
anthropological study of Europe and the Scottish Outer Hebrides, and the
development of techniques that promote critical thinking in the classroom.
Her most recent book is *Scottish Crofters: A Historical Ethnography of a
Celtic Village*, published in 1990.